Communication Skills

A Practical Guide to Improving Your Social Intelligence, Presentation, Persuasion and Public Speaking Skills

Positive Psychology Coaching Series

Copyright © 2016 by Ian Tuhovsky

Author's blog: www.mindfulnessforsuccess.com

Please be aware that every e-book and "short read" I publish is written truly by me, with thoroughly researched content 100% of the time. Unfortunately, there's a huge number of low quality, cheaply outsourced spam titles on the Kindle non-fiction market these days, created by various internet marketing companies. **I don't tolerate these books. I want to provide you with high quality, so if you think that one of my books/short reads can be improved in any way, please contact me at:**

contact@mindfulnessforsuccess.com

I will be very happy to hear from you, because that's who I write my books for!

Table of Contents:

Introduction.. 4

Part I: The Right Attitude and a Little Bit about Emotions....................... 10

Chapter 1: How Do Our Mental Filters Operate?.............................13

Chapter 2: A Map Is Not Actual Terrain 16

Chapter 3: Eight Most Important Questions You Should Ask Yourself 21

Chapter 4: How to Express Anger and Avoid Conflicts 28

Chapter 5: Smile 32

Part II: Communication Skills.. 34

Chapter 6: The Most Common Communication Obstacles 34

Chapter 7: 5 Most Basic and Crucial Conversational Fixes 42

Chapter 8: How to Deal with Difficult People............................... 44

Chapter 9: Phrases to Purge from Your Dictionary (and What to Substitute Them with)... 60

Chapter 10: Verbal Dexterity 66

Chapter 11: The Subtle Art of Giving Feedback............................. 73

Chapter 12: How to Become a Master of the Sharp Retort 78

Chapter 13: How to Have Unique and Memorable Conversations.............. 84

Chapter 14: Rapport, the Art of Excellent Communication......................91

Chapter 15: How to Use Metaphors to Communicate Better 101

Chapter 16: Metaprograms.. 106

Chapter 17: Meta Model 112

Chapter 18: Eye Accessing Cues 118

Chapter 19: How to Predict Future Behaviors 123

Chapter 20: How to Finally Start Remembering Names? 125

Chapter 21: 16 Ways to Have a Great Public Presentation 129

Chapter 22: Create Unique Personality in Business 137

Bonus Chapter: Effective Networking................................... 140

Conclusion 145

My Free Gift to You 147

Hey there like-minded friends, let's get connected! 148

Recommended Reading for You.. 149

About The Author 158

Introduction

It's one of the most important abilities in life, but you won't really learn it at school. There are not too many teachers on this crucial subject, but everyone has to go through the learning process and pass exams many times in their lives. There are no TV programs about it, although it is used by everyone, everywhere, all the time. The survival of a species depends on its quality, and the better particular animals or tribes master it, the more dominant they become over others. During a major part of most people's lives, it's automatic and not fully aware.

Effective communication—**exactly what makes human beings dominant on this blue planet.**

It is said that speech is silver, but silence is gold. Still, few will argue about the great power of words, either spoken or written.

In my personal experience, lack of communication skills is exactly what ruins most peoples' lives. If you don't know how to communicate properly, you are going to have problems both in your intimate and family relationships. You are going to be ineffective in work and business situations. It's going to be troublesome managing employees or getting what you want from your boss or your clients on a daily basis. Overall, I'd say effective communication is like an engine oil that makes your life run smoothly, getting you wherever you want to be. **There are very few areas in life in which you can succeed in the long run without this crucial skill.** Obviously, there are also other factors influencing the quality of your career (knowledge, huge network of contacts, experience, professional approach, proper education), relationships (soft skills, self-confidence, emotional intelligence) and other areas, but it's quite clear that all of your investments in the quality of communication, in improving its standards, learning new abilities or patterns and taking it to an entirely new level, **lead directly to improvement in your self-confidence, soft skills, career, relationships and your entire life's quality.**

Have you ever considered **how many times you intuitively felt that maybe you lost something important or crucial, simply because you unwittingly said or did something which put somebody off?** Maybe it was an unfortunate word,

bad formulation, inappropriate joke, forgotten name, huge misinterpretation, an awkward conversation or a strange tone of your voice? Maybe you assumed that you knew exactly what a particular concept meant for another person and you stopped asking questions? Maybe you asked so many questions, you practically started an interrogation? Maybe you could not listen carefully or could not stay silent for a moment? How many times have you wanted to achieve something, negotiate better terms or ask for a promotion and failed miserably? **It's time to put that to an end with the help of this book.**

Personally, I have had some serious trouble with accurate and effective communication during my lifetime, particularly back in my childhood, teenage and early college years. On the one hand, people usually liked me; I had a bunch of good friends and was rather a social kind of kid. On the other hand, I can't even count how many times I flunked really important exams in my life because of the inability to send precise messages, listen carefully, perceive what others were telling me without judgements or adjust what I wanted to say so my colleagues could understand what I really meant. I would also lose my chances for a second date with girls I liked too many times because I never knew when to shut up, stop "being funny and cool," and just start listening instead. I unwittingly offended some very stringent teachers or professors a few times because I could not see the world or a given problem from their perspective (which, obviously, resulted in VERY hard times for me, both on lessons and on exam sessions). I did not know how to deal with my parents and family during arguments and conflicts, how to maintain business contacts and, what the heck, I even got fired twice because of my lame communication skills and lack of intuition in conversations. At certain point I almost hit rock bottom. I lost my job, my health was bad, I ended my long-term relationship, depleted my bank accounts to make a few very bad investments and got in a really deep mess. That's when I promised myself I would learn from my mistakes, gather myself together and rebound.

I kept my promise. My self-development journey started, exploded and I never stopped my quest of self-betterment. I started reading TONS of books and watching LOADS of DVD's about many different subjects, which I decided to master in a few years' time. Sales, startups, soft-skills, meditation, emotional intelligence, eastern philosophy, NLP ... verbal communication was one of those crucial topics. In this book, I will share with you all the most important things I learned during my journey, so you don't have to commit the same errors and make the same costly mistakes. I learned it the hard way, **so you don't have to!**

Verbal communication is the most basic kind of communication among people. It has two forms: oral and written. Effectiveness of the former, on which I'm focusing in this book (although not exclusively, you will also have a chance to learn about non-verbal communication), is primarily influenced by fluency of speech and skillset of a sender, accentuation of particular parts of a message, confirmation from a receiver and paraphrasing of the received information in order to make sure that the real intent was understood correctly.

When talking about verbal communication skills, I mean certain competencies which include **knowledge, abilities** and **attitude**. On top of that there's **experience**, which makes applying effective communication patterns possible.

To explain it simply, only by applying **knowledge** and practicing certain **abilities** by having the right **attitude** is it possible to improve quality of your communication skills.

Quality is infinite as an indicator. This simply means that if you keep on working on the improvement of your communication competences, you will be constantly strengthening the quality of your career, relationships, social skills and your entire life, ad infinitum. **There are hardly any limits in terms of what you can learn and how much you can improve your social interactions.**

There's only one condition. Every single day you need to ask yourself this question:

What can I do even better, more efficiently, differently and more effectively?

It will make you think about the effectiveness and both strong and weak sides of your communication each and every day. During this process, you have to be both honest and forbearing with yourself, particularly when dealing with some deficiencies you are aware of. If you decide to deceive yourself, then you're just wasting your time. On the other hand, you need to stop beating yourself up. It will just block your mind and lead you astray. You need to be aware of one thing in particular: we, human beings, are often the strictest and harshest critics of ourselves, so if you are stuck on thinking, "What did I do wrong?", you will surely open the Pandora's Box in your own mind. Whenever you ask yourself a question formed this way, you are holding yourself back instead of developing and stimulating your mindset. So, again, the question you need to constantly ask yourself isn't, "What did I do wrong?" It is, "**What can I do even better, more simply, differently and more effectively to improve my communication with other people?**"

It is extremely important for you to constantly analyze your communication style and pay attention to communication patterns you use. You need to become aware of these things and find motivation to work on your personal development, improving the quality of your life.

The first steps of this journey are: awareness (knowledge of your strong and weak points—what to improve, what not to do and what to show) and motivation. The bad news is only you can work these two things out for yourself. Nobody else can do it for you. The good thing, however, is whether you want it or not, everything you read in this book applies to your everyday life. The power to change it for the better lies in your hands.

So, if you decide to take up the challenge and invest your time and energy in developing your communication skills, then you have just taken your first step to an entirely new quality of life. Stay persistent and you will be amazed at how fast and easily you can achieve things which just a while ago seemed far out of reach. Before we begin, let me expand a little bit on verbal communication (understood as **what** we say + **when, why** and **how** we say it) vs. body language and nonverbal communication.

Verbal vs. Non-Verbal Communication – A Little Debunking

Most participants of interpersonal communication skills, negotiations or influence trainings have probably heard at some point that the way of speaking is responsible for 38% of overall communication, spoken content (what we talk about) is 7% and body language is 55%. Maybe you have also seen it on TV or read about it on the internet. In 1967, Albert Mehrabian published the results of two surveys. Based on these results, he came up with the proportions between elements of communication as described above.

What most people don't know is that the results of the survey made by Mehrabian and his team[1] were generalized and simplified. For their experiment, they chose a group of people for the purpose of making two comparisons of various aspects of communication: the influence of tone of voice on the verbal message and the relationship between facial expressions and way of speaking. These proportions came from the compilation of results of both comparisons (which is one of the subjects of criticism). Other critics also point to the fact that the group consisted only of women, there was fragmentary focus only on relations between words and facial expressions, and so on. Mehrabian's survey concerned the relationship between verbal and non-verbal communication while expressing opinions, showing feelings and attitudes, where the goal was to check how each of these elements influences a positive reception of a speaker (seeing a speaker as a friendly vs. unfriendly person). In summary, the scheme tells us that the total proportions of the "sympathy factor" = 7% content + 38% verbal message (soft skills, use of language, rate of speaking, etc.) + 55% body language. All literal apprehensions of this graph can easily be seen as over interpretations. You can come across many allegations that 7% for content is definitely too little. This is not the main message of this survey, though. If **the proportions themselves are not really accurate and important**, then what is the essence of this experiment? It pointed to the fact that the effective communication consists of two inseparable elements of communication: verbal and non-verbal.

The "7%-38%-55%" rule can be seen as the metaphor of effective and efficient communication, which MUST contain the care of both verbal and non-verbal components, connected in a smart and congruent way. Lack or inaccuracy of both verbal and non-verbal message will essentially limit the effectiveness of communication and proper reception of the transmitted message. Non-verbal messages influence understanding and reception of verbal messages in a very crucial way. The proportions defined in this experiment are not permanent—they can change along with the context of communication, for example: a conversation between two people while in a business meeting, casual chatter between two friends, telephone conversations and so on. They are based on the study of facial expressions versus the

---

[1] Mehrabian, Albert; Wiener, Morton (1967). Decoding of Inconsistent Communications. *Journal of Personality and Social Psychology 6 (1)*: 109–114
Mehrabian, Albert; Ferris, Susan R. (1967). Inference of Attitudes from Nonverbal Communication in Two Channels. *Journal of Consulting Psychology 31 (3)*: 248–252

whole spectrum of non-verbal communication (postures, gestures, change of skin tones under influence of emotions, outward appearance and so on).

Non-verbal messages complement verbal messages, being nonspecific. Non-verbal communication is imprecise, whereas verbal communication is precise, so only both of these aspects used together properly will decide the overall quality of communication. **Effective communication is a verbal communication supported by congruent non-verbal messages** (tone of voice, facial expression, posture, gestures, etc.). **The congruence between these two elements is what makes communication truly effective.**

Now that we've covered all this, let's start learning how to change your life for the better!

Part I: The Right Attitude and a Little Bit about Emotions

Communication does not only consist of techniques. Above all else, it is the way of thinking about and seeing the world around you. A change in attitude towards everything that surrounds us, rather than solely using certain techniques, is the source of the biggest changes in our life.

Acceptance of this new attitude and seeing the world through entirely different filters can significantly change your behavior in many situations. Instead of reacting impulsively and emotionally, you will act more effectively and more constructively, always seeking for solutions and mutual agreement. Get to know these assumptions thoroughly and think how they apply to your life. It is important to consider how your behavior will change after you accept a particular way of seeing the world.

1. Everybody Has a Different Map of the World

It does not matter what this world actually is. We each get to know it by our senses: eyes, ears, taste, touch, smell. Due to the constraints of our brain, we can process only a small part of all impulses our environment constantly sends us. Each bit of information is processed by different filters: culture, language, beliefs, values, experiences. **Every human being has their own filters, which differs from the next person's.**

That is the reason why every person sees reality individually. Everyone perceives the same situation differently and can interpret the same words divergently. *We all live in our own, unique realities made by sensual impressions and individual experiences.*

What does such a view of the world give you? Firstly, you need to know that you can solve your problems by changing your own filters. You can change your beliefs, values and the way you see the world. It will make you change at a deep level. Secondly, getting to know a map of the world of another human being is the key to understanding them. When you truly realize and understand that everyone can see particular things totally differently than you do, it will be much easier for you to create healthy relationships. You will read more about maps and filters later in this book.

2. There Are Positive Intentions Behind Every Human Behavior

According to that concept, our every behavior is the result of good intentions. Even when we do something we are not proud of, we probably made that choice because it was **the best choice for us at the given moment**. It is extremely important to understand this concept if you want to change yourself and adapt new important behaviors. Remember that your old, unwanted behaviors were caused by the fact that your brain saw a positive intention for you in them. We are simply doing the best we can with the skillset we currently have. If anyone who has ever treated you poorly (your friend, co-worker, stranger, family member), could instead have treated you with respect and love, while receiving the same from you and having their needs met, they would do that. We all would, as that's how we are programmed—to give and receive love, fulfilling our needs at the same time. When someone's not doing that and behaving in a way we don't like, it's not natural. They're probably suffering, and that's what makes them hurt other people, and the reason for that is just **they don't get it**. They don't have the skillset to cope with the situation, they don't have the right tools, or they don't know how to use them. Very often, when you change your perspective, the things you look at literally change.

It is also very useful in relationships with other people. Always try to guess the basis of other humans' behavior. Think, "They are innocent, and they did the best they could in their current situation." Even if they aren't innocent, it will give you a much better understanding of their intentions, and open up the possibility of much better communication and also give them the opportunity to respond kindly and in a more constructive way.

3. It Is Impossible Not to Communicate

Everything you represent is some form of communication. In the process of communication, the non-verbal message and your voice play very important roles. Both verbal and non-verbal messages are always sent to trigger some kind of reaction of a receiver. The way in which a receiver reacts depends on the message you send and the way you did it. You are responsible for the understanding or misunderstanding of your words by a receiver. That is why you have to make sure the information you send is the same that the receiver gets.

For me, familiarization with these basic assumptions was a great foundation for getting to know more about the art of effective communication. Moreover, it gives you a picture of what self-development and the art of communication actually are. It is not necessarily a set of psychological techniques and tools, but a model of wise change for the better. Even now, I often come back to these assumptions and remind myself what is worth remembering.

Communication with other people is one of the most precious abilities among our vast array of interpersonal skills. Unfortunately as time goes by, some of these abilities, once learned, stop developing, stay on the same level, or can even diminish. There is, however, some good news—your ability to communicate can grow along with your life experience. That growth does not come easily though, especially for people who lack awareness of what to change as well as an openness for eventual change.

Chapter 1: How Do Our Mental Filters Operate?

Every single piece of information that comes from our environment goes through mental filters we all have in our minds. The realization of their existence is the first step towards working on your approach and attitude. A change of your attitude and mindset is the most effective route to a positive revolution in your personal growth.

How exactly does it work? **All your senses are your first filter.** They themselves already delete part of information about reality. When you are watching the world around you, you are limited by how the human brain is constructed. You do not perceive all of the physical phenomena with the naked eye—you can't see the gravity, sound waves, infrared light, UV waves, radio waves, Wi-Fi, microwaves, radiation, etc. You do not see reality as it truly is. What you see is only an interpretation, produced by your brain.

You have probably had a chance to see this illustration at some point:

Very famous picture. Duck or rabbit? Depending on who's looking at the picture, both answers might be right. When I first saw it at the age of five, I could just see the duck. It all depends on the angle and distance at which you are looking at it, your expectations and mental filters by which your mind is operating at the moment. How about this photo? Who's that?

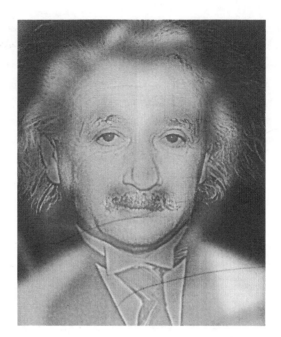

Albert Einstein or Marilyn Monroe? Depending on the lighting, the distance from which you are looking, condition of your sight, your expectations and mental filters or how wide your eyelids are open, you can see both. Do you see where this is going? We can't observe reality objectively.

Honestly, your way of seeing the world might be very far from the truth. Maybe brains of other species see a more exact reflection of reality? Perhaps a dog's brain is closer to perceiving the true nature of the world, despite the fact it sees it totally differently than a human? We have absolutely no evidence that states that it is our species that sees the world the way it really is, although we have many proofs that we can't see, hear, feel or sense even a tiny bit of what many animals can.

The other filters are acquired during life. These are **experiences,** which create your personality right from your birth, and also **values**, indoctrinated into your mind for many years by your parents, friends, education system and the rest of society.

There are your ambitions and expectations, **and most importantly, your beliefs about the world.** They create the way in which you see the world, your own life, opportunities and relationships with other people. If you believe that the world is a cruel and insidious place, you will behave like that is the absolute and only truth. It will give you a lot of unpleasant emotions and experiences. If your belief is that the world is a wonderful and beautiful place full of helpful people, your thoughts, emotions, self-talk, relationships and entire life will be totally different.

Every belief Is a Source of Specific Behaviors

Let's assume for a moment that you believe that every human is a liar who only wants to take advantage of you. Having such a belief, imagine how would you behave in a new company with new co-workers around you or trying to negotiate a new business deal?

Let's now change a filter and say that you truly believe that people love to make new friends and that everyone has something special in themselves. How will your behavior look then? How different will it be if you change only one of your beliefs so dramatically?

If you want to make a change in how your sensory filters operate, you can only do it by taking stimulants. By intoxicating your brain, you make it perceive reality very differently. You've probably had a chance to notice that after drinking too many beers, the world appears to be quite different (until the painful morning!).

The most important thing is you can easily change how the "second group" of your filters (mental filters) operate. You can change your way of referring to your past experiences. You can change your expectations towards the future. You can change your beliefs about the world that surrounds you and about other people. You can even change your deeply rooted values and your personal statement.

These adjustments cause the biggest and the most profound changes in your emotions, habits and communicational behaviors. They allow you to reach really deep into your consciousness and truly transform yourself. Instead of changing particular behaviors, you can start by changing your beliefs. Lots of people in this world (maybe even the majority) hold onto beliefs that not only don't help them, but simply hurt them and hold them back from real happiness and fulfillment.

A different way of seeing the world means a completely different life. Remember that you always have a pair of "mental glasses" on your nose. These glasses can be black and a source of unhappiness, but they can also be colorful, which will make your life much more passionate and much easier.

Chapter 2: A Map Is Not Actual Terrain

As you already know from first few sections of this book, every human has their own map of reality, which is not reality itself. Understanding of this concept will give you huge possibilities of development. You will start seeing the world and relationships with other people very differently, more in depth and in accordance with reality.

What is a map of reality? It is nothing else but a mental reflection of the world that surrounds us. As I mentioned before, you do not see the world how it objectively is in reality, but you perceive it through a set of filters: experiences, senses, beliefs and values. All of these create your unique, subjective map of reality.

Our mind is forced to select crucial information from a great number of stimuli, and every human has a particular algorithm, according to which the most important information is selected. Hence it's impossible to perceive the objective world. What you see is the reality that has already been filtered—all stimuli from the outer world are carefully preselected.

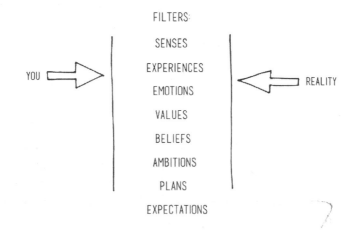

FILTERS:
SENSES
EXPERIENCES
EMOTIONS
VALUES
BELIEFS
AMBITIONS
PLANS
EXPECTATIONS

YOU ⇒ ⇐ REALITY

When you accept and understand it, you notice that every human being has a different map of the world. Eventually you'll come to the realization that every person on this planet has different life experiences, different beliefs, different values and expectations. Interpretation of the same information may be **completely different** when made by different people. **There is no one objective truth.**

Everyone is right according to their own map of the world.

Let me give you a few examples which will allow you to better grasp that concept. For starters, let's take Japanese manga comics. What is this kind of comic book for you? What does that word mean to you? For a manga enthusiast, the word "comics" probably has very emotional meaning which automatically brings a smile to their face. It may even be one of the most important words in their lives! For someone else, the term "comic book" may mean a bundle of paper worth close to nothing. Both individuals have different maps of the world, and for that second person it may be really difficult to understand the *otaku*'s map of reality. They could argue for hours whether manga comics are cool and interesting or maybe lame and boring, but what sense does it make? Someone might want pay exorbitant amounts of money for a single quirky painting, an old car which barely works, a postage stamp, a book so old you can't even read it anymore or anything else. Someone else might be wondering for weeks what's so special about an old copper fork from the 17th century when you can buy a new one for pennies. Who's right? Both of them. They just have different mental filters.

Here's another example. Has one of your colleagues ever heard something completely differently than the way you had intended in your mind? It's happened to me many times, and I could never understand why it was happening. It turns out that one simple message can have a completely different meaning for different people. In one person, the word "love" can cause dreaminess, in another it can cause pain and negative emotions. Therefore, you should always choose your messages carefully and take your colleague's map of reality into serious consideration.

Here's another situation. Because of the thick fog, a return flight from France to the United States is cancelled. What is happening at the airport? Over a dozen people jump with joy because they have an extra day to spend in this beautiful country. Some people are completely neutral—for them, nothing bad happened, but on the other hand, they are not sure what to do and how their families will react. Another group of people is desperate; they have important business meetings in the USA a few hours later. Some other people will be infuriated, because for them it will be their second canceled flight in two weeks. Exactly the same event—different people, different maps, different reactions.

Maps in Practice

I think that you can already see what this is about. Here comes the question: **how exactly can you use this?**

First of all, you should come to the realization that the way you live and whether you think that your life is good or not depends only on the kind of maps of reality you have. You see, most "happy people" are not happy just because only good things happen to them all the time. Just like some other people are frustrated all the time not just because they constantly stumble over sad and painful things. It happens because these happy people as well as those frustrated ones filter their reality in a particular way. If you have a belief that the world is a bad and sad place, that is how you will feel all the time. You will limit your perception of reality only to the bad aspects of your life and you won't be able to really notice all the good things that happen to you, simply because you can't focus on everything at once. You will filter the good emotions out at your own demand.

Having said that, let me tell you about one extremely important thing. There's a gap in time between event and response. Between, for instance, someone saying something mean to you and you giving them a response. Do you want to know what really happens during that time? Do we stop and think about how should we answer? It depends; sometimes we don't really think about our replies. Do we take time to think about what just happened? Maybe.

But what ALWAYS happens is we stop and **think who we are. Either consciously or subconsciously, it can happen in a fraction of a second. The way we react to this situation is simply a reflection of who we think we are**. We tend to think that we say and do what we say and do to other people because they did something to us. But that is not true. **It has nothing to do with what happened.** What people do and say to us has nothing to do with us at all. Therefore, we need to remember that everything we say and do is reflection of who we think we are and what we believe. What people say to you—it's about them. When you say anything, it's about you. It reflects who you are. **It's all about the way we are perceiving the events, the reality.**

There were times in my life when whenever someone was mean to me (saying, for instance, that I'm too skinny, too pale, too short, untalented or that I will never amount to anything), I would react neurotically and either aggressively or passively (blaming myself for not fitting into other people's vision of me). After I started working on myself, my self-confidence and my list of achievements got bigger and I attained totally different and new self-perception. Now, whenever someone is mean to me, I mostly don't give a crap. Depending on the context and situation, when it's possible to do so, I simply ignore it like someone would ignore a tiny, silent fruit fly on the other side of the room. Anything people say to you **doesn't have any meaning except for the meaning you give it.**

I've read three different books about people who survived Nazi concentration camps and Soviet gulags during World War II. Despite the fact they were treated inhumanly, cruelly, and their torturers attempted to smother their will to live at every moment possible, what all of these people had in common is they did not respond as these things were happening to them. They responded in a completely different way, reflecting their belief of who they really were. At the end of one of these books, there was a touching and eye-opening quotation from an extermination camp survivor's secret diary, later found by American soldiers. It was a twenty years young Polish girl who wrote,

> "It's my eighty-sixth day at the camp. I lost probably about 20 kilograms, I can see my every single bone and there are bruises on every centimeter of my body, but I'm still alive, which makes me really grateful. I also shared my bowl of grass soup with a starving little Jewish child, and the Nazis didn't notice. Today I was looking at Nazi soldiers. Poor people, they are watching us from behind these metal bars. If I'm behind the bars, so they are. We can't leave this place, and so they can't until their vain mission is accomplished. Locked in this prison of foolish human pride and self-conceit, and they think we are the only ones trapped in here."

All of these people (Polish girl, Russian soldier and Dutch-Jewish professor) in all three books did exactly the same thing to make their wall against the hell. They disconnected what happened to them with how they interpreted this situation. That's why the biblical story of Jesus Christ, no matter what your religion is or if you're a non-religious person, is so powerful to so many people. As The Bible says, Jesus was whipped, humiliated, spat on, kicked, made to carry his heavy cross and then crucified, but he never reacted if that was happening to him—he acted according to whom he believed he was—God's son. It doesn't matter if you're religious person or an atheist, you ought to see the ever-lasting wisdom beneath these stories and apply them into your daily life.

This change of beliefs or way of seeing your experiences will allow you to filter reality completely differently. The assumption that a map is not actual terrain is extremely helpful in social interactions and building relationships with people. Now, before you judge someone's behavior, you will remember that it comes from a different map of the reality that person has. If you want to create a strong relationship with another person, first get to know their map and then try to empathize with it. You will be able to understand their emotions, needs, behaviors and experiences at a much deeper level.

This concept also shows you that proving you are right doesn't usually make any sense. In the past, once in a while, I felt the need to argue with other people about who was right. I always tried to show them rational arguments and concrete proof and I could not stop wondering how someone could be so wrong about something. In reality, it was just like I had a map of New York and they had a map of Los Angeles and we would argue for hours whether the harbor was in the west or in the south of the map.

Think about how much energy you lost in your life for such pointless arguments. Now, when you know that everyone has their own map of the world and sees reality differently, through individual prisms, it should be much easier to understand that very rarely there is such a thing as objective truth and being one hundred percent right about something. Everyone is right in their own model of reality and if you want to improve your communication skills, you have to really think about it. After all, you can say, "OK, on my map the harbor is in the west, and on yours it's in the north. It doesn't matter as we have different maps. Let's find the right map together so we can finally find the damn harbor!"

Remember, there are as many maps of reality as people in the world. Make your map the most beneficial for yourself and respect other people's maps, without forcing them to use yours. This is one of the most important concepts in family therapy, psychology of communication, Neuro-Linguistic Programming and many other different schools of psychology, sociology and social dynamics. I will tell you more about this particular concept and how to make practical use of it later in this book, in chapters called "Rapport, the Art of Excellent Communication," "Metaprograms" and "Meta Model."

Chapter 3: Eight Most Important Questions You Should Ask Yourself

As we speak about right attitude, before proceeding to the verbal communication tools, let's now reflect on the most important rules and the essential knowledge about traits of an effective communicator, emotional intelligence and the right approach to the process of communication.

1. Is What You Say Possible to Realize?

Everything you say must be possible to realize—that is the first rule. If not, then the verbal message cannot be done and makes no sense. Let me explain. When you hear: "Forget about the number 4," or, "Don't think about anything green," you are not able to do it, because the process of forgetting is impossible (you can't just forget about something in a second, on demand, can you?). Such a command has exactly the opposite effect—a person thinks more about what they are supposed to forget, and reinforces the information which they wanted to delete or behaviors they wanted to stop. Do you see the pattern now? It is similar to common sandbox and playground comments parents so often tell their children: "Be nice" (or any other adjective). The verb "to be" is unworkable, because it is impossible not "to be" when you're alive. A child can't really understand this concept, which frustrates both the child and their parent. Instead of throwing out vague words, specify **exactly what** the matter is, and make sure that it is possible to perform a constructive action to have a concrete physical result.

2. Is What You Say Precisely Formulated?

"Be nice!" "Behave!" "You better motivate yourself!" Can you tell exactly what these sentences mean? No—they lack precision, and hence can be understood in too many different ways. In effect, it is almost a guarantee of an execution of your message far from your expectations. For example: instead of saying meaningless, "Be nice!", tell your child **precisely** what you are expecting, like, "Put the car on the shelf, where the other toys are." Rather than, "Behave yourself!", say, "Speak more quietly, please."

Do not demand "motivation" from anyone, because it does not really precisely show any solutions and doesn't point to anything in particular. Instead you could tell someone to straighten their back up, speak louder and talk about a specific goal or situation that makes them enthusiastic and excited. **Anything you say must be precisely formulated—that is rule number two.**

3. Is What You Say Positively Formulated?

Imagine that you ask someone if they'd like something to drink, or if they would like to have a coffee. The answer is "no." You propose a tea and the answer is the same.

- "Orange juice?"

- "No."

- "Glass of bourbon?"

- "No."

How much time will it take until you get irritated? Negation in itself is reactive—it applies to the already existing reality without constructive creation of the future, which leaves your interlocutor without a possibility of solving the problem. It brings especially negative consequences for small children, who hearing what they are not supposed to do are not able to create a proactive attitude for seeking solutions in themselves. It is because **our brain does not really recognize negations**—a proposition not to think about pink elephants will end up with failure, because what you hear (despite the negation), the brain will process anyway. Next time, when someone tells you, "I do not want to get at you, but..." you will know that they most probably want to get at you. Instead of saying to your employee: "Don't respond to a customer that way," explain **how exactly** you want that person to respond. **Rule number three: what you say must be positively formulated.**

4. Are You Talking to Others, or to Yourself?

"Understand it," "Know what, I'm talking to you," "You feel me" ... Other people cannot understand you in the way you want to be understood, because that can only be done by yourself. No one can be responsible for the mental and emotional processes of other people, as in the end it is you who decides about what you think and how you feel (apart from whether your interlocutor triggers and stimulates it or not). Because of different "mental filters", it is not possible for other people to always entirely understand what you mean, or "feel" you the way you want it.

They can understand you based on how they imagine what you say, and how they feel and interpret it, according to their own cognitive filters. If you can really and deeply understand yourself (that can be the hard part), when you know what exactly you want to communicate and you feel yourself, then communicating your message to the other person will be not only possible, but easy. **The rule number four is to remember to always take responsibility for yourself.**

5. Is What You Say a "Mind Reading" or a Description of Measurable Facts?

- "I can see that you are sad!"

- *("No, you can just see tears in my eyes. I was cutting an onion.")*

- "I know what you are going to say!"

- *("No, you don't. You are just reminding yourself what I said in a similar situation last time.")*

- "This picture tells me you were not too happy back then."

- *("No, pictures do not speak. You just interpret them this way, and then you put your interpretation on the picture. It is an attribution error[2] (pictures are not able to*

---

[2] Gilbert, D.T., & Malone, P.S., (1995). The correspondence bias. Psychological Bulletin, 117, 21-38.

speak) and a projection bias[34] (thinking that what we think about the reality is in fact identical with what our interlocutor thinks).)"

Correct reading of mental processes in reality is very hard (until today, psychology has never found unequivocal solutions concerning things like reliable reading of body language) and almost always close-to-impossible in everyday communication and usual circumstances, even after thorough CIA training, no matter what you watch in your criminal-drama TV series. It is also estimated that the majority of e-mail communication (or online chat communication) is usually deformed, meaning that the reception of a message by the receiver is usually different than intention of its author. Have you ever got in an argument because you didn't include the smiley emoticon, or omitted an abbreviation (e.g. IMHO)?

Description of facts has an objective character and when you treat your own judgement as an objective description of reality, it often leads to many conflicts.

- "You look nervous!"

- "No, I am not..."

- "Don't tell me you're not! I can see you are!"

- "What's your point? I just told you I'm not nervous."

- "Why are you responding to me that way and rising your voice? Why are you so nervous?!"

- "FOR GOD'S SAKE, I TOLD YOU ALREADY. I'M NOT NERVOUS!!!"

- "STOP BEING SO ANGRY AND SHOUTING AT ME!!!"

And so it escalates...

---

[3] Loewenstein, G.; O'Donoghue, T.; Rabin, M. (1 November 2003). "Projection Bias in Predicting Future Utility". *The Quarterly Journal of Economics* **118** (4): 1209–1248

[4] Harvey, J.H., Town, J.P., & Yarkin, K.L. (1981). How fundamental is "the fundamental attribution error"? Journal of Personality and Social Psychology, 40(2), 346-349.

Remember about the fifth rule of conscious communication—always describe **measurable facts** instead of trying to read minds.

6. Does What You Say Describe What You Feel or Attack Your Interlocutor?

Offending your interlocutors usually leads to activation of defense mechanisms in them, which helps them defend their self-image. Telling your partner: "You don't love me!" will probably end with the negation, "It's not true. I love you!" retaliation, then "You constantly jump at me!" and eventually escalation of conflict ("Here we go again, how many times can you make up problems that don't even exist? When will you stop behaving like a little boy/girl?!"). Instead of attacking your interlocutor, it is more beneficial to tell them about your own feelings, which have an educational and informative character and are safe for your interlocutor's integrity and self-image. In reference to the above example, instead of, "You don't love me!", a much more effective and wiser message would be, "Yesterday, when you said that I looked bad in that dress, I felt very sad!" If the interlocutor says that they did not have that on their mind, it is worth explaining: "I understand and I'm glad that your intentions were different. Nevertheless, I understood it that way. Next time, could you say that in a different way, for example ...?"

This rule (sixth) saves you from unnecessary conflicts, relationship problems and waste of time and energy. Remember: always describe your feelings without attacking and offending your interlocutor. It will just lead you astray.

7. Does What You Say Concern a Person or Their Behaviors?

Our opinions about others are always generalized, and we usually reduce them to a common denominator. It's always an evaluation of some kind, and it does not matter if it's positive ("You are very smart") or negative ("You are so stupid!"), it always builds a biased and unreal picture of our interlocutors in their (and often our) minds. It's unreal, because everyone has moments when they act either in a very intelligent or really dumb manner. Moreover, it always depends on the observer's opinion, because after all, there are no "one hundred percent objective criteria" of intelligence and stupidity (even complex IQ and EQ tests or extremities like Darwin Awards can't be viewed objectively in all cases). These unreal or biased pictures build a particular type of biased self-esteem (or self-doubts), and the message itself describes the external reality for your interlocutor (even if biased), what makes any changes almost impossible. What do I mean by that? For instance, when someone isn't seemingly very intelligent and has never acted too smart in many areas of life according to your opinion, then you can't really transplant their brain, can you? However, what you CAN do is refer to their behaviors, because these—as opposed to inborn capabilities or personality traits—are quite easy to change. Additionally, it's much harder to offend someone when relating to their behavior only. Instead of, "You are stupid," say: "When you go to meet your client next time, please, read much more about their company so you really know what you are talking about, okay?" Instead of, "You are so intelligent!" it's sometimes better to say: "When you expressed your opinion about that book yesterday, it was so immersive and well-detailed, you really inspired me to read it!" Rule number seven teaches us to **express opinions about people's behaviors, not about them in general.**

8. Does What You Say Have Hidden Intentions?

"Honey, weren't there any prettier dresses in the shop?" is not a question about availability of other dresses, but a negative comment judging that particular one, or more likely, the person wearing it. The words, "And what do you think, for God's sake?!" do not mean that you want to know other persons' opinion, you just want to show your own frustration. Messages with double meaning, in which a told content differs from the real speaker's intentions, lower the level of trust of adult interlocutors, and won't be understood by most children. Because the building of a relationship without trust is not possible, the more direct and straightforward your messages are, the bigger the possibility that what you want to transmit will be received properly and positively. Of course by "direct" I don't mean harsh or explicit. Social correctness, emotional intelligence, empathy and sensitivity have to be taken into consideration.

So the eighth rule is to say directly what you want communicate.

Implementation of all of the above rules requires a systematic practice and awareness. Some of the most basic communication mistakes (for example: telling your children or employees what they shouldn't do instead of what they should do, or sending vague, bland messages devoid of any real meaning) are so common that despite their dysfunctionality, they are perceived as something "normal" by most people. Fortunately, every ability can be trained, and the best idea is to focus on one of these obstacles/dysfunctionalities for a minimum of one week. As soon as you see improvement, you can proceed to another one and so on, until all the rules are applied. The amount of misunderstandings and conflicts will surely be greatly decreased.

Chapter 4: How to Express Anger and Avoid Conflicts

Wrath and anger are both destructive and creative emotions. They can motivate us, remove blindfolds from our eyes and give us lots of strength when directed properly, but their destructive nature is revealed whenever we suppress our feelings. How should we express these emotions to use them for creation of a healthy communication with other people, instead of sudden, chaotic outbursts of anger?

In our Western society it is normal to suppress wrath, anger and other bad emotions. It results in big amounts of unleashed energy residing in us, which sooner or later erupts like a lethal volcano.

Surveys conducted by Dr. Robert W. Levenson from UC Berkeley Institute of Psychology indicate that suppression of emotional expression does not contribute to reduction of experienced emotional intensity, but rather overstimulates and overloads our neural systems. This leads to reduction of immunity and health problems[5]. Suppressed emotions always manage to find their way out eventually[6].

To understand how anger works, we must realize the difference between a stimulus and a cause. Every emotion is a result of our thoughts. The cause of each emotional state lies in our thinking. It is one of the basic assumptions of cognitive-behavioral therapy. The behavior of another person which we didn't like is then a stimulus, that activates (indicates, reminds us of) a real cause (a thought that starts to haunt us again).

When your partner does not call you for a long time, you can feel anger and accuse them that they don't care about you. However, if you look deeply at the real cause of your anger, you could realize that you simply need more love signals from your partner. Subconsciously, you decided to treat the stimulus (no phone call) as the cause. This is

---

[5] http://conium.org/~ucbpl/docs/42-Emotional%20suppression93.pdf

[6] http://ist-socrates.berkeley.edu/~ucbpl/docs/51-Hiding%20Feelings97.pdf

how we transfer the responsibility for our bad emotions to the external world instead of taking a better look at ourselves, our emotions, thoughts, feelings and needs.

When we express anger we usually interpret a stimulus as a cause and we blame the other person for our anger. Feeling that a certain behavior should change or end, we accuse them, saying that they did something wrong and the next time they have to do it differently.

In result, our interlocutor is raising the shield and going into defensive mode. It's a normal, usual reaction. Where there is an attack, there is also a defense. The stronger the attack is, the stronger the defensive reaction.

As soon as your interlocutor starts defending themselves, they are not able to understand what the problem really comes down to. Their priority will now be to push the accusations away and to resolve the conflict as soon as possible (usually not in the healthiest way possible, but the quickest, to release the tension they feel). They also won't be able to change their behavior, even if you communicate to them how extremely important it is to you (probably yelling or crying at the same time, as the conflict escalates).

The basic mistake most people commit when they are angry is blaming the other person for what and how they feel. They are not aware that anger really tells them about themselves. On the surface, it seems like a stimulus is a cause of our anger and bad emotions...and the real reason stays unknown.

The source of anger always lies in our thinking, beliefs and attitude. Our needs, expectations and judgments. If you feel anger, it very often means that some of your needs remain unfulfilled. When you choose yelling and accusations as a method of expressing this emotion, you'll have unnecessary conflict instead of solution, and your relationship with the other person will possibly get worse.

So what should you do when these intense emotions occur? Treat them as an alarm, a sign pointing to a certain unsolved problem. When the siren howls, direct all your attention inwards. Why do I feel anger? What exactly make me so angry? What am I missing, which makes me feel this way? What do I need?

Such insight and finding answers to these questions is not too easy when we feel like we want to fight and pour these bad emotions on the other person. It is very important, however, to stop for a while, take a deep breath, and give yourself a few moments to observe what is going on inside of you.

When you lose control of yourself under the influence of bad emotions, the explicit expression of your anger can be very tempting, and even pleasant in a way. Holding it in may require some inner strength, but when you manage to push the "STOP" button, it's sometimes better to leave your room, house or the apartment before the anger explodes and the conflict escalates. Then, you need just a few moments and some good questions to ask yourself and the emotions will start to evaporate. Working on a constructive dialogue, you can return with a desire to talk in a calm manner and to solve the case in a healthier, more efficient way.

Have you even wondered why, in a frenzy of anger, we have such a huge need to throw unpleasant words at others and simply make them feel bad? Why can pouring this anger and psychical bullying be so pleasant?

Simply, we want them to become aware of the pain we think they made us feel. We want to give these bad emotions back so that they admit their mistake, submit and surrender. We want them to finally change their behavior.

The problem is that when someone thinks they have done something wrong, they will not even have the opportunity to empathize with your pain. They will allocate all of their energy to defend themselves.

Therefore, there is no point in blaming others when we feel bad. It makes no sense at all on a practical level of reason. If we want to solve the matter constructively, we have to allow that person to understand what is going on inside of us, how we really feel. To express your anger wisely, it is worth it to restrain yourself from throwing swear words, plates, cutlery and photo frames.

When you accuse someone of something, the accused person has two possible choices. To take your words personally (which will make them feel hopeless and restrain them from changing their behavior) or to reject them (which won't change their behavior either).

If you really want someone to change their behavior, remember, **they must feel the need themselves**. It can happen ONLY when they feel no need to defend themselves and when you explain them very calmly and clearly what exactly you feel, why you feel that and what your needs are.

Let's recap quickly:

1. Take a pause. Stop for a moment and take a breath. Put aside any accusations against the other person.

2. Be aware of thoughts which are the source of anger. Reflect on them deeply. What judgment, opinion or belief in your head makes you feel the way you feel?

3. Understand your needs. If you already know the thought being the source of anger, consider what need this thought comes from. What specifically are you missing?

4. Express your needs. Do not judge the other person. Talk only about your feelings, which appeared due to the particular behavior of that person.

If you want to express your anger in a healthy way and use it to create agreement and build better relationships, stop blaming others for your feelings and direct the beam of consciousness on your emotions and needs.

Learn how to constructively communicate these needs, to help others understand what you feel and where your anger comes from. This will help them to change their own behavior according to what is important to you.

How would you estimate your level of control over the intense, devastating emotions?

Chapter 5: Smile

Why do we like to laugh so much? What happens in the brain when you smile?

1. Your smile is controlled by two groups of muscles—the major zygomatic muscles and *orbicularis oculi*. These first run on the sides of the face, connecting with the corners of your mouth. When you smile, they reveal the teeth and raise the corners of your mouth. *Orbicularis oculi* are responsible for closing the eyelids. They are also responsible for the wrinkles in the corners of your eyes.

The movement of zygomatic muscles can be controlled by us. We do this when we want to smile artificially. *Orbicularis oculi* work independently of our will and appear **only when we laugh honestly.** So if you want to know if someone laughs for real or artificially—look at the sides of their eyes. During artificial laughter, only their mouth laughs.

2. A smile is contagious. Scientists have discovered the "mirror neurons" in our brains which are responsible for recognizing the emotions on other people's faces. After such a recognition, they turn on the areas of our brain responsible for the same emotions (sometimes it's enough to look at a photo of a smiling baby or watch a short clip with someone laughing in it). When we see a smile on another person's face, we can also start to smile very easily—we automatically feel joy, so smiling affects the behaviors of other people and their reactions on us. Also, **when we laugh often, people see us as more friendly, nicer and happier.**

3. Laughter is good for your health. Smiling positively affects your breathing. When we laugh, we breathe faster, and this is a great exercise for the diaphragm and throat. It also increases the oxygenation of the blood and betters your blood flow. According to neurologist Henri Rubinstein, one minute of honest laughter equals 45 minutes of deep relaxation.

4. The hormone of happiness. Laughter stimulates the secretion of endorphins, hormones in the brain. These are of similar chemical composition to morphine and heroin, but they calm and strengthen your immune system. The release of endorphins greatly improves our well-being.

5. The mere act of smiling, even artificial, causes the release of endorphins in the brain. Activity of the muscles responsible for smiling is so strongly associated with our well-being that it works both ways. So if you want to feel better in a second, just smile a couple of times, even if you do not have the desire to. Try it yourself, even now.

6. Social smile. Research shows that we laugh more often when we're in the company of other people rather than when we are alone. Robert Provine says that only 15% of our laughter comes from the amusement of jokes! There is wisdom to that—so many times I barely smiled when reading a joke alone at home, but when I heard the same joke while with a group of people, I cried out loud with unstoppable laughter. It turns out that laughter has an important social function; it's the way to forge relationships.

Conclusions? They are probably obvious. **Smile more often to improve your communication skills!** Your brain will be functioning much better, and other people will see you as a more sociable and friendly person. What's more, you will also improve their humor and you will feel much better in the process.

Part II: Communication Skills

Chapter 6: The Most Common Communication Obstacles

The ability of effective communication consists of:

1. Understanding of others (and showing it)
2. Clear expression of oneself
3. Imposing an influence on others
4. Active listening
5. Asking open and detailed questions
6. Taking care of our own needs and goals during a conversation
7. Exchanging opinions in a non-conflicting way

Get to Know Your Obstacles!

If you want to improve your communication skills, you need to recognize your limits first and really think about all the things holding you back while interacting with other people.

A good idea is to ask the people you see most about what you should improve in yourself (or even change totally) when it comes to your way of communicating. It might appear as a strange idea at first, but believe me, it's one of the most effective ways of inner transformation. Your friends, family or coworkers (interlocutors in general) may often see some aspects of your communication (sometimes as subtle as tone of voice, facial expression, etc.) which are totally invisible and unconscious to you. Now, let me tell you about the most common obstacles on your way to becoming an effective communicator. Take a moment to reflect at each of these points very deeply and honestly. No need to deceive yourself. Answer yourself: are you doing these things often?

Playing a Judge

Do you often tell others how you think they are or how they should be? Perhaps you are certain that your way of perceiving the world is the only correct way? If you tend to show judging behaviors, you may have a tendency to interpret your interlocutor's messages through mental filters of stereotypes or your own beliefs and experiences as you are the only one with the right to be right, which can turn out to be wrong and unfair.

Feeling the Need to Finish Sentences for Others

Often, while talking with others, you interrupt and practically finish the whole sentence instead of letting your interlocutor do it. It is very frustrating for people around you and can make them unwilling to continue conversation, even if you are not told this directly. In some instances, if it happens constantly, it can even contribute to ending of your relationships because a listener does not try to analyze what a sender is trying to say. If you are a frequent interrupter, **do everything you can** to stop this tendency. You could, for example, imagine yourself as a journalist taking an interview with a VIP, in serious need to gain as much information as possible about the other person.

Uncle Good Advice

When you share your observations and give others advice, you almost always feel like you can surely help them or contribute to solving their problems. Step back and take a moment to think about how you feel when other people are constantly giving you their advice (especially unwanted advice). How does it make you feel? Instead of playing a good uncle and giving your "helpful tips" to everyone ("If I were you, I would..."), try putting yourself in your interlocutor's place or situation and reflecting on how you would feel when something like that happened to you. Eventually, you can give advice if that's your field of expertise or you're asked for it. Only just enough advice and not too much, only an honest attempt to understand your interlocutor deeply and nothing more. As often as possible, avoid playing a role of a wise sage or oracle, and try to lead a conversation the way your interlocutors are able to solve the problem by themselves.

Moralizer

A little bit similar to "Uncle Good Advice," but even worse as it's totally pointless. Does your style of conversation have features of a moralizer? "Good and honest men do not act that way!" "Every intelligent man put in your place…" "You can't just say that to people!" "Who do you think you are?" "How can you listen to this kind of nasty music?" "How can you wear these bright colored clothes all the time? If I were you…" "One day you will see!" "When I was your age I never…!" Are these the sentences that you say often? If the answer is yes, really think about what you want to achieve by saying these things. It is the most irritating and the least effective way of communication. Try to avoid that kind of sentence as often as possible, unless you want to be perceived as a hunchbacked grumpy old aunt with a never-ending headache, chronic back pain and a fiery hatred for cute small animals.

Being "The Talker"

Maybe you have a tendency for too many frequent, excessive utterances, meaning that your mouth rarely shuts. On one hand, it can be a feature of your openness, knowledge or high intelligence. On the other hand, such need for a constant self-expression can be overwhelming for others.

This feature is not too frequently required in everyday situations (only sometimes, when you first meet someone, when they're shy and you want to kick start the talk), and makes it really hard to receive genuine info about other people (and also feedback about yourself) during the conversation. Too much excessive talking from your side can be really discouraging in the early stages of relationships, and too often you may wonder why a selling transaction was cancelled or somebody avoids contacting you. It really feels like hanging out with a parrot or an actor rehearsing his annoying monologue for the fiftieth time before a big play. This was my big obstacle and the reason I was able to date many nice girls back in my high school days, but without a chance for a second or third meeting. I simply talked way too much and rarely listened to them, but it took me many wrecked first impressions and sleepless nights to figure that out. They probably felt like they were having dinner or a walk with a TV screen. Many men have problems with that. Even today I can talk A LOT and once I start firing words, I often have to force myself to stop, thinking, "Easy, you will have time to say all these things, but not yet. You are not here alone! Chill out, dude."

People Who Don't Let You Speak

As opposite to above, you may have a tendency for submission in relationships with others. Do you have the impression that others are not interested in your opinion? Do you often find yourself in situations where your interlocutor takes advantage of your attention and does not let you speak? Think about the reason beneath such situations.

Maybe have a bad opinion about yourself ("I have nothing interesting to say"). Maybe you are afraid of other people's reactions when you want to interrupt a conversation or simply add to it. Do not let that happen. You have the same right to speak as others have. If you feel bad during a conversation (someone is overwhelming you by their talking), just stop them, politely tell them about it or try to change the subject. Don't waste your time and energy.

The key phrase is, "So, you're telling me..." It's a great navigational tool to use in conversations with people who tend to often jump from one topic to another and talk about one hundred different things in a matter of few minutes. I have this business partner who tends to very often lose track in his conversations, and he really is a big talker. If you took him to a business meeting and asked him to quickly tell you how he got into the retail business and what his background was, he would tell you something like: "Well, that's an interesting question. In 1979 I was a military school dropout, before that I originally wanted to become a pilot because I always wanted to be paid for playing with grown-man toys, and you know, the military planes are so fascinating. I don't know if you've heard about the new project for US army stealth-planes, they can fly above the stratosphere and they're equipped with the newest..." and then he would tell you everything he knows about military, soldiers, their families, their friends and dogs, and probably he would love to tell you a story longer than all nine seasons of *How I Met Your Mother* put together.

What you need to do to politely interrupt in that situation is to take any of the last sentence that person said and repeat it back, prefacing it with, "So, you're telling me."

So if my friend got to that point, I would tell him something like: "So, you're telling me that these new planes can fly really high, right?"

And normally when you say something like that to people, they respond with saying, "Yes, I was telling you that...but why did you ask me?" and then they go back right on the track. "Ah yes, I'm a mechanical engineer." Or if they forget the original question, you just need to repeat it and they get right to the answer you wanted to hear, but they are not offended that you are interrupted them, because you interrupted them while showing that you are listening to them carefully at the same time. As an effective communicator, you will sometimes have to lead the conversation where it needs to go.

Comforting Words

There is nothing wrong with comforting someone, at least at first glance. When we comfort someone we have good intentions, and we want to show that a certain situation is not so bad and it will get better. But clichés like: "Don't worry, there will be a new day tomorrow," "Others may be in a worse situation than you are," or a very common saying, "Keep your head up!" usually bring exactly the opposite effect. These sentences usually show a low level of communication abilities. Remove them from your list of usual reactions. What you can do instead is this simple process: first of all, acknowledge what and why this person is feeling. That might be, for example: "Really?! That's a horrible thing to have to go through!" That's what people expect to hear rather than, "It's not bad," or, "Don't worry," which would mean they are exaggerating, overreacting or creating an artificial problem. The next thing you should say instead of using cliché phrases is something like: "I just want you to know I'm here for you, and I will be here for you until you overcome this situation," or, "Know that you can count on me if it ever happens to you again."

Losing Focus

Do you often find yourself distracted when listening to others? Perhaps it is also difficult for you to stay concentrated or focus on something for longer periods of time? Maybe you often show your impatience nonverbally. If that's the case, you should dedicate a good bit of time to improving your focus.

By mastering the ability of concentration on what other people say to you, you get more valuable information which enables you to focus on the real benefits of contacting with others and also allows you to be there, in the moment, which not only makes you much more likeable, but also more effective as a communicator. Thanks to this, you also make an impression of a trustworthy and understanding person, and thereby you build deeper relationships with others.

Let's now recap quickly what you just learned about basic communication obstacles. To communicate effectively and avoid distraction tendencies mentioned above, you have to remember some basic rules:

1. Do not judge others; try to separate your own interpretations from what your interlocutor really said.
2. Listen patiently to the entire conversation, and paraphrase often—the latter makes you rehearse what you have just been told and keeps your mind from wandering away. Not only that, but it also creates a very good impression of a genuine listener.
3. Instead of handing out advice all the time, pay attention and show readiness to find something interesting in your conversation.
4. Give people you talk to a chance to show their beliefs, even if they are quite different to yours. Do not show disapproval in the form of moralizing, such as "Not bad, but when I was your age...," or, "But I would do it differently and more efficiently," etc.
5. Try to notice your interlocutor's subtle emotional reactions (you have to actually look at them when you talk) to know if your utterances are overly expanded or not.
6. Remember that you have the same right to express yourself as everyone else. If you feel overwhelmed, don't stop yourself from telling people who talk too much that you disapprove of this.
7. Instead of comforting with cheesy clichés, just learn to show interest and approval to your interlocutor.
8. Work on your concentration (e.g. by applying regular meditation and relaxation techniques), and endeavor to understand other people's real intentions.
9. If possible, communicate face to face. Nowadays, we have a plague of Facebook and e-mail quarrels and serious arguments, or even break-ups. When you don't

see who you're talking to, you can't recognize their emotions. Written communication is also often dishonest: people often accuse somebody of something or offend them and read the answer whenever they want to (or never), not giving the other person a chance for a direct reaction. Poor and weak...but unfortunately more and more common. It's so easy to hide beneath your computer screen, but it's hard to say these things face to face.

There is a saying, "Everybody wants to grow, but nobody wants to change." When it comes to communication abilities, it is worth the effort to open oneself for such a change.

The oldest public opinion research institute in the world, Gallup Institute, conducted a very interesting survey. It concerned the most irritating and nerve-wracking speaking habits. Below, I would like to show you the results the research gained, from the least irritating to the most irritating factor:

Place 11. Speaking with a foreign accent

Place 10. Too high-pitched tone, squeaky voice

Place 9. Grammar mistakes or incorrect pronunciation of words

Place 8. Rapid talking

Place 7. Groaning, nasal speaking voice

Place 6. The use of fillers like "eeeer," "uhmm," "you know" (It's a common illness; people are usually just afraid to take a pause and allow themselves to be totally silent for a while, which is way better than constant "uuhmmm"-ing and "you know"-ing.)

Place 5. Colorless, bland, and monotonous speaking manner or voice

Place 4. Overly loud talking

Place 3. Muttering or overly quiet talking

Place 2. Swearing or frequent usage of overly explicit vocabulary

Place 1. Interrupting when someone else is talking

So we have another important obstacle, the final one.

Despite of someone's irritating voice, swearing or muttering, it is **<u>INTERRUPTING</u>** **which is <u>THE MAIN VERBAL FACTOR</u> beneath IRRITATION AND UNSUCCESSFUL CONVERSATIONS.**

Your conversation should look like talking on **walkie-talkie** or **CB radio** in the car. **When one person talks, the other one listens.** When one of side pushes the "transmit" button and also starts talking, they obviously won't be able to hear what their interlocutor has just said, and might have lost important information about what's on the road ahead of them. Every time you talk to someone, try to remind yourself of the "CB radio" example.

These bad verbal habits are often a significant barrier in our everyday conversations. If you avoid them whenever you can, you will see a huge improvement in your social life and career.

Now, take a quick look at all these obstacles again and ask yourself if you can recognize your patterns of speaking in them. Do as much as you can to eliminate them forever.

Chapter 7: 5 Most Basic and Crucial Conversational Fixes

Let me now expand a little bit on what we learned in the previous chapter and tell you about the 5 most powerful and easy-to-apply conversational improvements you need to start using.

Stop for a Moment

One of the most basic and crucial things to do, which most people aren't doing in conversations, is to PAUSE before replying. A short pause (2-5 seconds) after a person stops talking is a very smart and savvy thing to do. When you pause, you accomplish 3 goals at the same time.

First of all, you avoid the risk of interrupting if the person is just taking a breath before continuing. The second benefit is that you show the other person that you're taking careful consideration by not jumping in with your own comments at the earliest opportunity. The last benefit is that you actually hear the other person better. The words will soak into deeper level of your mind and you will understand what they are really saying with greater clarity. By pausing, you mark yourself as a great person to talk to.

Ask for Clarification

Another tactic you can utilize in order to greatly improve your communication skills is to ask for clarification. Never assume that you fully understand what the other person is saying. Instead, if you have any doubt at all, ask: "What do you mean," or, "What do you mean exactly?" Then just pause and wait.

It's one of the biggest assets I know to lead and control a conversation. When you ask "What/how do you mean?", the other person can't stop himself or herself from answering more extensively. You can then follow up with other open-ended questions and keep the conversation going.

Paraphrase

Another very good idea is to paraphrase the speaker's words in your own words. You can nod and smile and then say, "Let me see if I understand you correctly. What you're saying is this..."—and then you repeat it back in your own words.

By paraphrasing the speaker's words you're demonstrating that you're genuinely paying attention and making every effort to understand his or her thoughts and feelings. It's also the best way to politely interrupt and lead the conversation back on the right track.

Listen More, Talk Less

You need to know that listening builds trust. The more you listen to another person, the more they trust and believe in you. Listening also builds self-esteem—when you're listening to somebody, their self-esteem will naturally increase, and they will feel more valuable, respected and just better. Finally, listening will also build your focus; your mind can process words at 500-600 words per minute, and we can only talk at about 150 per minute. It takes real effort to keep your thoughts focused on other people's words. If you do not practice self-discipline in conversation, your mind will wander in one hundred different directions. In other words, by learning to listen well, you actually develop your own character and your own personality.

Three-Second Look

This one is actually a useful addition to the "stop for a moment" fix, which you can use in many different situations. When you suspect that someone is not telling you the entire truth, hiding something or stretching the facts, you need to just stop talking. After they finish their sentence, look them directly and deeply into the eyes, for three seconds nonstop, completely silent. You can also tilt your head a little bit forward. Since we are programmed and conditioned to deal with this kind of pressurized situation rather badly and lying can be very difficult, it usually ends in your interlocutor breaking down and telling you the truth, giving more details, etc. It can be also used when dealing with difficult people, for example, when you don't to answer their nosy questions.

Chapter 8: How to Deal with Difficult People

Dealing with difficult people is extremely important, especially in the corporate world and any other kind of professional life, when you can't afford to just ignore them, and also in everyday life.

In this chapter you are going to read about the most popular types of difficult people and how to deal with them easily and professionally, like the polished communicator you want to be. Let us start with the most important principles you should always keep in your mind:

1. **Avoid trying to change these people.** First of all, their behavioral patterns are usually well-rooted and it would require at least a few psychotherapy sessions to change their behavior. So, unless you are an experienced psychotherapist or hypnotherapist, don't try it. It's a little bit like an amateur trying to dismantle a bomb: ineffective and careless. Moreover, even the best professional in the world can't change someone who doesn't want it and doesn't allow it. All you can do is to point out the annoying behavioral pattern, but it's not your job to transform these people.

2. **Set your boundaries.** You need to let these people know that you will respect them, but you also want to be treated with respect and won't accept anything else. Don't tolerate shouting and pathological arguments in public situations or other forms of disrespect. If necessary, tell them that you need to remove yourself from the situation and just leave. A good idea might also be to wait until they calm down and are ready to talk more temperately. Teach and condition others how to treat you and never settle for less than you deserve.

3. **Remember about different mental maps and positive intentions behind every behavior.** Even though you don't agree with someone's viewpoint, you need to realize that there must be some reason behind their

annoying actions. Realize that it must be difficult to be stuck in such a negative situation with anger and other bad emotions. Empathy is helpful if you want to deescalate a frenzied situation. Sometimes all these people want is to be heard or paid undivided attention to, they just lack the skills to communicate it in an effective way. Also, don't take things personally. These people's behaviors show their own level of self-development, emotional intelligence and communication skills, not yours. They might be tired, traumatized or in the middle of a really difficult life situation.

4. **Don't talk too much.** When dealing with difficult people and their irritating behaviors, it's often a good idea to make your verbal messages brief and concise. You should also have a timeframe in your head and know how long you're willing to be a part of a discussion. Instead of talking about things like "attitude" (it might be taken as a personal offence), focus on certain behaviors these people represent.

5. **Focus on behavior, not people.** Instead of saying things like, "Michael, you are a liar!", rather say, "Michael, we both know that what's been said is far from reality." Having said that, you should always use a passive voice when having difficult conversations. Instead of telling someone what you want them to do, say what you want to have done, e.g., "Michael, I need that report done by the end of the day!", not, "Michael, you need to finish the report by the end of the day!" Active voice: here's what you did to me. Passive voice: here's what was done to me.

6. **Focus on the most crucial things.** When you are facing difficult peoples' behaviors, they always want you to engage with them in a way they imagined or are used to. When someone does not fall in their pattern, they usually get beaten off their track. Remember: don't take their bait and never engage more than you have to. What gets rewarded gets repeated. Another important thing is to often use the broken record technique, using exactly the same words/phrases, which sends the clear signal: "I'm not easy to throw off my game. I know how to stay on message."

7. **Use "difficult people" silver bullets.** First and foremost, use boundary statements. They are usually based on, "Would you like A or would you like B (you can't have both)?" In this instance, when somebody is trying to get your help while being verbally aggressive, you might say, "Sir, I do want to help you

and address your problem, but not if you're going to keep your voice raised." Then, you would use the so-called empowering statement, e.g., "Would you like to take a few minutes before we continue our conversation, or have a cup of tea, or are you ready to continue now?" Another smart thing to do is to use the so-called "preemptive attack," which comes down to alerting someone that what you're going to say is going to aggravate the person a little bit. The more you jump around and try to hide it, the more difficult it will be for you to eventually say, and as hard to acknowledge for your conversation partner. The more you warn your interlocutor that what you're saying is difficult, the less difficult it will be for them. So you can say, "I'm terribly sorry Mr. Smith. I know it will be extremely frustrating to you, but your car won't be ready today. We will have to lend you a different model and your car will be ready tomorrow morning." That lets the person know that you understand the situation is bad and also saves you even more frustration by the end of conversation. The last wise thing to do is to validate people, even the difficult ones. Even phrases like, "I can see why," "I understand you were really angry," or, "Oh, that's really bad!" can be helpful (unless you say something like, "I understand exactly how you feel"—no, you don't!). Ability to validate anyone in your conversations while being truthful is a great communication skill, not only useful to deal with difficult people.

8. **You can also use suggestions.** For example: "Bob, if we do XYZ, how do you think it might affect you?" By saying this, you show people you are interested in their opinion. Often there's much tension relieved when we let people express their thoughts. People become much more open when they know you are really listening and paying attention to what they think. When you get the answer, you should say something like: "If I understand you correctly, you think (here use the same words they spoke). I considered that and here's how I see it..." At the end, you need to quickly add, "Does that make sense?" By doing that you show that you too have been thinking about alternative solutions and resolving the conflict, and that their idea is one worth considering, and that you are interested in their opinion. It permits the person to say if they agree or not and opens communication process to more constructive discussion. That's something always worth trying.

Another important thing is body language. You can't send a firm message while your body is sending signals that you are being passive. Here's what you need to remember in this context.

- Find your tone of power. Here's how you do that: simply look down at your feet and go, "Mmmhmmmm." This sound should be resonating, strong and firm. When you localize it, you need to speak in a slow and steady tone. When you speak too quickly, you project an image of uncertainty and nervousness. People tend to listen more when you speak slowly. You also want to keep your tone within a small range, without going up and down too much. Of course, that only applies to difficult conversations, not your everyday chit-chats!

- Keep your head straight—don't tilt it. That's what dogs and other pets do when they want to show you they are playful and harmless. That's the same message you are sending when you tilt your head to the side. If you don't want to project an image of someone who's soft and easy to take advantage of, you want to lean slightly forward with your shoulders back and your chest out. You may also want to shift your head forward a little bit.

- Keep your eye contact. In normal conversations, you don't want to maintain eye contact for longer than 7 seconds, but during difficult conversations, you should maintain it much more intensely, which is going to send a message that you are strong and hard to knock down verbally.

- Get rid of physical things standing between you and the person you are communicating with. Physical obstacles contribute to conversational barriers. Again, remember that these bullet points are about difficult conversations, not normal communication.

How to Fully Disengage

Imagine that you are dealing with a difficult customer, your annoying boss or anyone else who is just eating at you and has gotten you off track. If you really want to let that go, instead of saying to yourself, "Let that go. Surrender to the moment. I'm at peace," which may be effective, but not in this kind of situation, you want to do this simple 3-step process. First of all, you want to start with disengaging physically. Many people grab a coffee, cigarette, beer or turn on the TV, but don't do that! Go for a walk! If you can find a place to stretch or do a few pushups, do it immediately! Go for a bike ride or exercise for 15 minutes. If you do it on a daily basis, you will notice that after you finish, you feel different. Exercise forces your body to release endorphins, which makes you feel good. Then, you need to disengage mentally. Begin with asking yourself, "What are the objective facts?" Then ask what your role and their role in this matter are, and what options you have. For instance, "They called me an imbecile!" That's their role. What's your role in this? If you think, "My role is nothing," you're wrong. It might be, "In fact, I believe what they said," or, "I feel disrespected and humiliated. I don't understand them," or, "I got too emotional and acted like a silly kid, throwing names back at them and now I feel dumb." That's your role in this. Lastly, consider your options. It might be, "I can just ignore it," "I can honestly talk to them about what happened," or, "I can stop seeing them," or, "I can just decide that it's OK they are calling me that, it's not really my problem." Once you have done that, you can disengage verbally. Most people can't disconnect from the problem at all. They store all the painful things inside them, take them home, watch TV with them, eat dinner with unfortunate events, and then go to bed, keeping them under their pillow. And it's not a funny thing. When you remember about these two steps, you can really change your behavior for the better. When you want to disengage verbally, always remember about different maps and the principle of good intentions. Remember that in fact, these people are innocent. It may sound silly, but the person who it helps most is really you. It's much easier to communicate effectively when you take these two simple steps beforehand and remember about positive intentions and different mind maps.

Coping with Passive-Aggressive People (The Snipers)

We've all had or will have to deal with passive-aggressive people at some point in our lives. Whenever someone is picking up on your specific behavior, giving you mean comments hidden behind snarky lines or a "joke," attacking you verbally using seemingly polite words and sugar-coating their offenses, they are being passive-aggressive. Some people do it just from time to time without bad intentions, but some act this way too much. Back in the day when I was working in an HR department, I bought myself a pair of cool marine-blue suit pants. I liked to wear them on special occasions, such as company meetings. There was one typically passive-aggressive guy named Christian who would always pick on them and say something like, "Hey Ian, how's your work in the car repair shop?" For a while it was quite funny and I didn't think repairing cars was a bad thing to do. However, he never stopped teasing me about it and it became more and more annoying. After two or three times, he would start asking me if I was going to change his tires, then he went even further and started calling me "lost postman," "fired mechanic" and "delivery boy." What I didn't know then was **you should always call these people out on their abusive behavior.** If they say mean things in public (and that's what they usually do), you need to address their behaviors in public. If you don't, they will continue doing it more and more aggressively. These people usually have some kind of problem associated with you, but either they are too scared and not strong enough to say it directly to you, or they can't do it in a given situation. There's what you should do.

1) Repeat what they said.

2) Clarify their behavior.

3) Ask a closed question to confirm or deny their intentions.

When that "blue pants" thing happened again, this time at a business conference in front of our entire department, I looked at him with a serious tone and facial expression and asked him, "Christian, when you asked me again at which discount store I bought my suit pants at and told me I looked like a delivery boy, what I'm thinking is that you are trying to belittle me in front of our co-workers. Is that what you are trying to do?" You simply want to repeat their behavior, clarify their intentions ("Was that your true intention?", "It is that what you wanted to do here?", etc.) and then ask them a closed question (yes/no) to call them on their actions and make them either confirm or deny their intention in a clear and professional way. These three simple steps tell these people that you're not going to engage in their "jokes," nor let them get away with what they are doing one more time.

Christian blushed, become awkwardly silent for a few seconds and said, "Oh... I'm really sorry, it was just this joke we had, you know..." Well, I didn't know. I just gave him a three-second silent look. Then he shut up for the rest of our meeting and never picked at me like that again. Of course, this was a professional situation and this guy was rather smart (he was probably jealous for some reason, maybe because I was given better projects). It's also possible that if you ask, "Are you trying to insult me?" someone replies something like, "YOU BET I AM!" As long as that person isn't actively aggressive, threatening you, etc., the best way to answer it is to ask, "Interesting, why would you do that?" and then go from there. People who ask more questions have more perceived power in the relationship than those who answer them.

Coping with Nosy and Challenging People

There are many kinds of very annoying and hard-to-deal-with behaviors in people. Let me tell you another work situation related story. In the very same office, there was this girl Kate. She was nice to talk to from time to time, but unfortunately she never knew neither when to stop asking questions nor where the boundaries were. Replies like, "Stop asking. I won't tell you," worked on her like red cloth works on a bull. Once, when I just finished talking to my boss on some strategic decisions in the HR department, she came to my cubicle and started asking me, "Why did she wanted to talk to you?" Obviously, it wasn't her business and I had lots of work to do. Knowing this girl was very stubborn, inquisitive and much into gossiping, I didn't feel like giving her a report on my conversation with the boss. The first time I ignored it and just kept typing on my computer. When she asked me her nosy question for the second time, I gave her the silent three-second look and asked her, "Why would you ask that?" "I'm just curious..." she replied. I smiled briefly and asked "...are you always this curious?" She got a bit surprised and then replied, "Well, uhmm, yes, usually." Again, I looked directly into her eyes for three seconds without saying anything and said she got a little bit unsettled. Then I stared at my computer screen again and asked, "What were we talking about?" Normally, at this point, everyone would probably understand that I didn't want to tell them anything, but she replied, "Huh? I just asked you what you and Isabelle were talking about." Again, I gave her the three-second look and asked the same question, "Are you always this curious?" She replied "...but you just asked me and I just told you!" And I asked her back, "Well, what were we talking about?" Guess what? Yes (or "oooh noo")! She asked me again! So I asked her why would she ask that and if she was always this curious, she got perplexed, turned on her toes and finally left me alone. You just learned a perfect technique you can use to deal with nosy, stubborn and challenging people! Again, I wouldn't advise you use it on your boss, but it will work with anyone on your level of the hierarchy. Don't worry, not all people are quite as stubborn Kate was, but this little trick worked even on her. This persistent broken record technique is really frustrating and effective when it comes to this type of person. Again, all you need to do is asking something like, "Why would you ask that?", then ask them a question regarding the answer they just gave you to make them taste their own sword and get them off their train of thought, e.g., "Is everything people do so interesting to you?" (Mind you that this question shouldn't be aggressive or mean. Actually, being very polite is much more confusing and works much better). Then, when you get your "yes" or "no" you ask, "What were we talking about?" to either change the topic or totally confuse the challenging person.

Coping with "Judges"

We all know people who feel the urgent need to judge others and make everybody listen to their comments on everyone and everything around them. Sometimes it might be a good idea to simply ignore it (non-reactive people have much bigger power in social relations), but sometimes enough is enough. Few know that dealing with this kind of person is actually not that difficult at all. All you have to do is repeat the judgement while super-exaggerating it, and then ask a distorted clarifying question. This simple, yet effective trick is something I actually learned from my mother.

I remember when I was a teenager, my mum had this colleague from her work, Ms. Jacqueline, that she sometimes invited over for a coffee. She was overall a nice person, but very much into judging others and criticizing everything and everyone way too often. Once she made a mistake and commented on my behavior ("The music he listens to is really aggressive and difficult to get along with!"). Then, fifteen minutes later, she told my mum that my sister, who was several years older than me, should have been married long ago. My mum probably had enough of her judgements that day and she said, "When you say you believe my daughter should have been married for a long time now, are you saying that she's too ugly or too dumb to find herself a decent man?" Ms. Jacqueline almost spilled her coffee on her pink dress, covered her mouth with an open hand and replied, "No...oh! My dear! That's not what I'm saying at all!" My mum just looked at her silently for a few seconds (I imagined laser beams firing from her irises) and then said, "By the way, it reminds me of that funny book I read in elementary school..." As far as I know, Ms. Jacqueline never commented on our family members again. You should've seen her face (I did as I was just stealing their heavenly chocolate cookies)! I just figured it out a few years later my mum actually used one of the most effective social-dynamic techniques without even knowing it.

That's what you can do when you feel that you are struggling with someone's annoying judgements. Repeat what they said and ask a clarifying question, exaggerating the whole thing. Then, give the person a clear three-second look and change the topic saying something like, "Now that you mention it, it reminds me about..." Again, you want to remain calm (or at least act like you are) and polite, but be straight-forward and serious (don't say it like their judgements are a funny joke). With some hard-case people you may have to do it two or three times, but believe me when I say they will get the message. That's the perfect way of dealing with these people in an eloquent, polished, and effective non-aggressive way.

Coping with "The Exploder"

The fancy sounding "Exploder" is a name for people who often lose their temper, yell and scream at other people or are just rude and nasty in general. People act like that for many different reasons, but usually it's because in the past, when they acted like that, other people would get intimidated and give them what they wanted. The number one reason difficult people are difficult is because it's **working** for them. The best technique you want to have in your pocket is called "DTU" – "Do the Unexpected." When aggressive people shout, get intense and into your face, they either expect you to start shouting back at them (usually not a good solution), or surrender and give up. When you do something else, they usually snap and lose their temper. One good idea is...to actually agree with them. This is one of the best "silver bullets" you can use when it comes to dealing with this kind of verbally aggressive person. Let's say that you are working in a bank, and one of your clients comes to you and starts yelling that his two dollars disappeared from his bank account due to some kind of online error. He says that he's so upset, it's thievery, a scandal, that he will call the police, the military, and an exorcist and sue you and all your family if you don't give him his two bucks. The best thing you can do in this kind of situation is to say something along the lines of, "Yes sir, you are right. I agree that two dollars is a substantial loss and an unacceptable error..." What you would do here is look for some nugget of rationality in their exploding madness. Remembering that everyone is using different mental maps, moral values, and acting according to different beliefs, you need to realize that behind all their unreasonable communication, they are usually upset about something that's easy to be upset about. When they start exploding, they usually expect a fight. By agreeing with them, you show them you are on their side, which allows you to solve the problem much faster.

Naturally, if you have these people in your social circle as colleagues or friends, you should do everything to avoid them as often as possible, if you can afford that.

If you really need to disagree with them eventually, start by agreeing (finding bits of rationality in their aggression, like stated above), and then, once they calm down, disagree constructively. If it's possible, you can put the blame/responsibility on someone else. For example, say, "If my boss was here, he might say..." and then express your disagreement. Then, ask a question. "How would you solve this problem?" or, "What would be the perfect solution for you here?" Listen to their answer and say something along the lines of, "Your idea is interesting, but I cannot agree with (repeat the exact spot of disagreement using their words)." For instance: "Your idea is creative and inspiring, but I cannot agree that five hundred dollars as a compensation would be a good fit for both sides of this dispute. But we don't have to agree on everything and we can work out another mutually agreeable solution, can't we?" Adding the "Can't we?" is very important. And then you need to stop and listen again. Then you push the idea that you can agree to and still get along, avoiding the disagreement and moving onto something more constructive and desirable.

Coping with "The Diverter"

Anyone constantly trying to divert your attention from the subject at hand to what everyone else does, etc. is called a "diverter." It could be a person in your company who usually says something along the lines of, "In my previous company we used to do this differently," or, "With our previous manager, we never..." It can also be a teenager who wants to go to a party, and when you don't allow it you hear something like, "But Jack's parents allow him to go!!" The solution here is simple. You need to remember this simple script: "The subject here is not XYZ; the subject is..."

So, for example, you might say: "The subject here is not what you did in your previous company; the subject is how we are going to deal with this project..." or, "We are not talking about Jack's parents and their parenting methods; we are talking about how far away that party is from our home and your big exam tomorrow." Of course, these people might also say different things like, "We could do that project better if only we had more people/more funds etc.," but it's essentially the same meaning. Again, you need to use "the subject is not" technique. So, in this instance you might reply, "I agree with that, but the subject is not what we could do with more funds we don't have right now. We are discussing what we can do in our actual position." Very simple, yet effective.

Coping with "The Steamroller (or Tank)"

Also called "hostile aggressive" by psychologists, steamrollers are people who try to run over you to get what they want. They try to overwhelm, bully and intimidate other people, often throwing in cutting remarks. They are mean and rude to you, intentionally and directly, verbally offending you and sometimes even threatening you, which sets them apart from "exploders". It's another type of person you shouldn't hang around with, but if you can't avoid it, here are some tips that will help you deal with this most difficult type of person. First of all, you need to remember that what these people are trying to do is to make you angry and lift your emotions to their level. You can't let them do it. You need to keep eye contact, stay calm and assertive. A good idea is to let them go and go at the beginning, and let them unwind. When they grow a little bit tired of attacking you, it's time to interrupt them. Imagine a boxer who is used to receive lots of punches into his chest and stomach, just to make his opponent exhausted and then—bang—KO! Let the steamroller to wear themselves out a little bit and then call them on their behavior. "Michael, wait a minute. I've been listening to you, now it's time for you to listen to what I have to say." Once you say something like this, they will probably...interrupt. You need to remain assertive and interrupt back. "Hey, I said hold on. I've been listening to what you have to say, and now it's my turn."

A very important thing is to determine whether this person normally acts like that, or if they're just now becoming extremely upset about something very stressful to them and want you to listen. If it's not their regular behavior, you should sometimes just listen and open yourself to a constructive dialogue. You need to also ask yourself whether there was a particular event that might have triggered their aggressive behavior. Usually you are not responsible for the actions and frustrations of steamrollers, even though they believe so, and you don't have to tolerate their rude behavior. When you can afford it, sometimes a good idea is to just ignore them without engaging and walk away, but if you can't, you need to turn conflict into communication. Again, here's how you do it:

- Give them enough time to run down.

- Grab their attention. You don't have to be overly polite, nor mean, rather assertive and abrupt. Speak up loud enough, from your diaphragm. Call them by using their first name, if possible and appropriate. Hold your head up so that your chin is pointed upwards. Straighten yourself up, hold your arms back and your chest up. Maintain eye contact.

- Try to get them to sit down. If you are seated when they get into the room, stand up to be on their level.

- State your opinion boldly, but not aggressively like they do. Use the facts.

- Avoid engaging, arguing or trying to get them down. Just express your opinion and do everything you can to end the conversation as soon as possible.

Coping with "The Complainer"

Positive-minded people see the world this way: It's not too sunny today. At least I won't get a sunburn again and won't have to use air conditioning. I guess I will stay home and read a great book!

Negative-minded people see the world this way: The weather sucks. It's cold, cloudy and I feel sleepy.

The Complainers see world this way: Oh no! The weather is horrible again! I wanted to take a walk, but now I'll end up cold, wet and I'll catch the flu for the fourth time this year. I will have to spend a few days in bed, and it's boring! I will also have to spend lots of my hard earned money to buy meds and maybe visit the doctor! This summer sucks! How the hell I'm supposed to enjoy it? It's so dark I can't even read without feeling sleepy. There's nothing interesting to do around here! And Bob just left town to visit his family and...

This type of people will always find a good reason to complain and will find a defect in everything. They will often want to make you believe it's your fault. By putting you on the defensive, they shift the responsibility for their own actions and emotions upon you. Here's how to deal with their endless whining and dragging everyone else's emotions down.

First of all, you need to realize what things don't work with complainers:

- Offering a solution/giving your advice or addressing their problem directly – they will usually start whining about your solution, the action they have to take, your attitude or about anything else on this planet.
- Trying to cheer them up or telling them to get it together – supposing their problem is trivial one way or another (even if it really is!) is highly ineffective.
- Complaining or criticizing their whining – see bullet point number one.
- Ignoring them – it will just cause the complaints to accumulate and then explode at you at once when you eventually meet them again.

- Here's what works:

    1. Instead of rolling your eyes or ignoring them, let them know that you're listening and seeing their problem. Something as simple as, "Yeah, traffic jams can be really intense and annoying sometimes!" can prove very helpful both for you and them.
    2. Complainers don't want cheering up, rather they want your attention and your empathy. Remember to be sincere when you say these things. If you're sarcastic or making fun out of it, the effect will be opposite.
    3. Remembering that everyone sees this world through different mental filters, you don't have to agree that their problems are really big, but remember that something seemingly small to you might indeed be a big problem to someone else, depending on their life situation, previous experiences, values brought from home, etc. So you either don't want to state that their problem isn't a problem or that it's enormous. Just acknowledge that there's a problem they are struggling with (even if you think there isn't one, or that wouldn't be a problem for you). You need to

let them know that you understand and acknowledge what they have said, but you shouldn't actively agree with them. It would just make them feel clean-handed and sometimes shift the responsibility for their emotions to you.

4. Listening and acknowledging their problem might not be a perfect fix which stops their complaints once and for all, but it surely slow things down, prevents the negative energy from accumulating, and gives both you and them some initial relief.

5. You need to be ready to interrupt them. Listen, understand their concern and them stop their utterance in a civil, polite but confident manner.

6. If there's a need, provide them with facts. State them without any comments, apologies or additional remarks.

7. If it's a workplace or a professional situation, you need to come up with practical questions and then proceed to problem solving. Complainers very often put their focus and attention on the past, but if you assign them a specific task they could to, it can often help. You can say something along the lines of, "Yes, these young guys from the marketing department can often get extremely annoying. I know exactly what you mean, but I hope you can endure it, soldier, because we totally have to have this project completed before five!"

8. Finish the utterance as soon as possible, politely letting them know that you have to get back to your things.

9. Remember that even everyday complainers sometimes come across things that are really hard to cope with, so if you think that someone might really struggle with something and their complaints are legitimate, you can show your empathy, followed by brief and targeted advice. In this case, it will probably be appreciated.

How to Stay on Track

Do you know the feeling when someone throws a cog into the wheels of your conversation, presentation or idea? When we're not trained in the art of effective communication, it's very easy to put us off, disarm our arguments or discourage us verbally from doing something. You need to be persistent in your message to achieve what you want. You need to show that you are not just another scared newbie, but a polished and effective communicator.

The ideas I will tell you about will instantly boost your self-confidence in situations where you are making a request for something, presenting your ideas or sharing your opinion in team projects. We let other people twist us in different directions just because we lack the tools to block their evasive answers. "The tools" really come down to three very simple and effective phrases which you can use when something is trying to get you off track. The three universal skeleton-key phrases are:

- That may be, but...

- I understand, however...

- I see your point, and...

You need to use them in front of your reply, and then repeat exactly the same words you said previously. Let's say that you are brainstorming the direction of your business with your partners and want to change your product's graphic design as you are certain that a change is needed at this point. You say, "Listen guys, we need to change our website because it's not easy to use for our customers. It looks like it stays in the 90's, loads slowly and shouts, 'DON'T BUY OUR PRODUCTS' directly in our customers' faces," to which one of your colleagues rolls his eyes and responds, "But we just changed it five years ago!" Then you need to respond, "I see your point, but we need to change our website because it's not easy to use for our customers." And he says, "Oh, you are being so very innovative these days, aren't you?" You say, "That may be, but we need to change our website because it's not easy to use for our customers." And then he goes: "You know we'll have to pay someone to do this?" And you, keeping your calm, collected and professional attitude use the phrase again: "I understand, however we need to change our website because it's not easy to use for our customers." This broken record technique along with these three skeleton-key phrases used in a row send a clear message: "Don't do that, man. I know what I want to achieve and it won't be so easy to put me off. I'm an effective communicator, not another scared little kid who's easy to distract."

Again, take note that I won't advise using it with people who are higher in the hierarchy than you are, for example your boss (of course it depends on the person and context, but you may want to balance pros and cons of doing it first), although it's extremely useful with people from the same level of the social ladder, having similar power and influence as you, or people who don't have any power over you, just trying to distract you from your goal for some reason.

Keep in mind that these strategies are no magic bullets. Yes, they can be extremely helpful, but since everyone's different, you need to view them more as a general rule of thumb. You need to learn these strategies and practice them until you feel comfortable using them in everyday situations. You can use them to cope with many difficult personalities in your life and gain more self-control and social control in many different situations.

The problem of coping with difficult and toxic people is as wide of a subject as psychology and sociology themselves, so I will probably write another whole book exclusively on this complex topic, where I'm going to cover all the types of difficult people distinguished by modern psychology with comprehensive descriptions, strategies and action steps. For now, the strategies and ideas I gave you on the most common difficult personality types will surely prove as a great help in your everyday communication!

When someone does something mean to you, it's about them, but when they do it another time, **it's usually about you**. Let me clarify: when people do something annoying over and over and over again, it's about you, because you are allowing that. What are you doing to award their behavior? There must be something. Look for that and try to ask yourself how you are rewarding their mean actions. It's difficult, but we can always do it when we know where to start. And we start from ourselves. Changing your behavior is the most effective thing you can do to deal better with difficult people, and all other kinds of people for that matter.

Chapter 9: Phrases to Purge from Your Dictionary (and What to Substitute Them with)

Both in work situations and at home, there are specific "phrases of highly ineffective communication" in our verbal repertoire which need to be eliminated completely, and substituted with different, wiser and harmless phrases. Many of them are so popular in our culture that you might be surprised to find you're using them on a daily basis. Let me now tell you about the most detrimental and useless things you could be saying in casual and professional situations and what to exchange them for.

Casual Situations/At Home/Relationships:

1. This one is big. I'm sure almost everyone has had the opportunity to hear it at some point in their lives. Yes, I'm talking about the infamous, cheesy and cliché "We need to talk" phrase. First of all, it creates lots of unnecessary tension even before the beginning of the conversation. Second of all, it has a very serious connotation in our culture, so instead of having a more relaxed conversation, you will create a more stressful and uptight atmosphere. Third of all, it simply sounds stupid, like a cheap C-class TV soap opera from the 80's my Grandma used to watch. "Romeo Alejandro Maria Antonio Rodriguez, how could you cheat on me with Esmeralda Rosalia Julia Desgaldo for the fiftieth time this very season!? We need to talk!" But that's my personal opinion. Point being that you really need to completely eliminate this phrase from your repertoire! What should you say instead? "I need your help." People like to help. Did you know that we tend to like people who we've helped before more than those who we haven't? That's actually one of techniques in social psychology—if you want someone to like you more, ask them to help you with a small task. Anyway, when you say so, you are triggering positive emotions in them, and they feel needed. They will also concentrate better on what you are trying to convey. It's a great start for a "serious conversation," which doesn't have to be perceived as such, being more relaxed and productive instead.

2. Another phrase which we often use when someone gets us off track, says something unexpected, or acts unusually is, "What's wrong with you?!" It's a good phrase if you really want to make someone feel bad, but if you want to solve a problem or difficult situation instead of annoying or hurting people, you need to erase it. No one likes to admit that there's something wrong with them, so don't ask, "Are you damaged in some way?" Instead ask, "What's bothering you?" Not only are you showing that you care about that person by saying this, but you're also avoiding creating an even more stressful and neurotic atmosphere. You're reframing the situation, pointing to a certain problem this person might have rather than to what might be wrong with them as a person. If the person still acts mean or withdrawn and says, for example, "Nothing..." while rolling their eyes, depending on the situation, you could kindly say, for example, "Well, okay. Remember that if you want to talk with me about something, my door is always open for you." Of course you can use different words, but you have to show that person that you are always there to listen to them. Sometimes you might receive a positive answer, e.g.: "Right... I'm just sleepy and irritated; I'm sorry for my grumpiness," or an answer pointing to a certain problem, "Yeah, always open for me, right! Last time I wanted to talk you just..." Either way, it gets you closer to the real problem and the solution.

3. Another crucial thing in our "Hall of Infamy," a phrase causing bad emotional response on a subconscious, biochemical level. It is: "You said *something*," or "But you just said..." Anytime you say something like this, you just make your interlocutor much more annoyed, irritated and angry. Remember the last time when someone tried to tell you that you did or said something you didn't, how did it feel? You probably instantly got pissed off or maybe even aggressive, right? The automatic response in your brain is resistance: "NOPE! I NEVER SAID THAT!" Even though you are 100% sure that person said something, it is always much smarter, classier and more effective to say, "I heard/I understood *something*. Let me clarify what I just heard before I respond, alright?" Phrases like these can totally change the result you get.

4. Let's now proceed to another cliché and very poor phrase which is very popular in our culture that we hear far too often. "It is what it is." What does it even mean? Nothing. It's empty, devoid of any meaning, hard to understand (especially for children) and very annoying thing to say. You could just as well say, "Buttons, haircombs, dumplings, scissors," "I like grapes so much," or, "My pajamas are well starched!" If you don't want to leave your interlocutors annoyed, confused and feeling ignored, you're better off saying, for instance: "I believe it's this way because it needs to be like that on this stage where we are right now," or maybe, "I believe all things are the way they should be at the moment, to make us stronger and..." Do everything to delete meaningless "It is what it is" from your conversations, especially when there's a tension or stress involved. It's a good thing to read in ancient Stoic philosophy scriptures, but not suitable for effective everyday communication.

5. Here's the last one I'm going to tell you about in this book. Anytime you say, "That doesn't make sense," the message your speakers will often perceive is really, "You don't make any sense." You really want to be more precise, at the same time avoiding stressful situations. Instead, say: "I don't understand..." for example: "I don't understand what you mean exactly by saying that..."

Professional Situations:

Let me now tell you about phrases which are sometimes socially accepted, but not suitable for polished, savvy and effective communicators. If you want to be perceived as a professional and achieve your goals easier and faster, you also need to eliminate them from your repertoire. Let's start with the first one:

1. "No problem!" How often do we hear it when someone does us a favor, in a shop, in the office, during a business meeting, etc.? While you might be surprised, as the phrase is extremely common in everyday life in English speaking countries (and not only), it actually implies that there was a problem attached to the thing they did (or we did). Since our brains don't really understand and can't perceive negations at subconscious level, and you don't want to subconsciously

communicate that there was or could be a problem with you doing someone a favor, it's much better to simply say, "You're welcome!" instead.

2. Very often, especially when being serviced at shops, we hear, "Do you want/do you need...?" (e.g.: "Do you want a bag?"). While you might think now, "I don't understand. What's wrong with saying it?" you have to know that, first of all, depending on the tone of voice and manner of speaking, "Do you need..." might be perceived as mean by some customers, especially when the vendor is repeating it for the fiftieth time that day, or is simply tired. Also, "Do you need" or "Do you want" sounds a little bit like a hidden remorse sometimes (stating that there's a problem with someone wanting something again). Second of all, customers are often asked only about their preference, not additional service with the help of these questions—e.g. if they like sugar in their tea or coffee—they already paid for it, so it just boils down to their preference. Instead, it's more universal and much more professional to say, "Would you like...?" Not only is it more kind, but also fits almost every situation possible.

3. Let's cover another one. The word is: "Unfair"—NEVER EVER use it in your working environment. The brutal truth is "fair" has nothing to do with work environments (and never has). The same goes for life in general. Whenever you go to your superior and say, "I don't believe I was treated fairly," or, "I think I was treated unfairly," what they think is probably, "Yeah, life is not fair indeed, sweetie pie." It's the best way to be perceived as a soft and unprofessional person. Instead you should say, for example, "I don't believe I was treated equally in this situation." No one ever promised work will be fair or life will be fair, but most people are rather sensitive when it comes to equal rights and chances. That's much more polished, suitable and useful in work situations and is less likely to lead to a failure.

4. Often, when we want to give our message bigger power, we use words like "really" or "very" as we think they will underline and bold our message and make it stronger or more influential. Very often it's the other way around—it's the elimination of words like "very" or "really" which makes our messages stronger and more polished. It's a very common problem for lots of women, as they tend

to use these words more often in their verbal messages, but also for many men. If you want to convey your messages more professionally in the workplace or in a business situation, stop using these words to supercharge what you're saying (they end up vague or poor sounding instead) and compose simple straightforward messages instead. What sounds more serious: "It's really dangerous!" or simply, "It's dangerous"?

5. "I can't deal with..." Never let anybody hear you saying that! It makes you appear as a helpless, neurotic or maybe even toxic "victim type" of person acting rather like a sulky teenager than an adult. It's ten times better to say instead, "I'm struggling dealing with..." On the top of that, you should also add a question for a contribution to this problem. For instance, let's say that you're talking to your manager about how your team operates and your annoying colleague: "Listen, Bob, I'm really struggling to deal with Mark's frequent unpredictable behaviors. Do you have some tips or advice for me on what can I do?" Not only does it show that you are a problem solver, but also instead of simply throwing your issues at other people, you ask them to contribute, which makes them feel needed and appreciated. It's a very professional and effective behavior.

6. Whenever someone is not behaving normally in a professional situation, you should avoid saying that they act "strange," "weird" or "funny." It can be perceived as a mean thing to say, or even an insult, that's for sure, but moreover, that doesn't sound professional and can make that person start acting even more extremely. Additionally, it's just your opinion you're giving, which is not always wanted, needed or positively perceived in many different work situations. Anytime you see that someone's behavior is unusual and they are not acting "normally," it's much better to say, "I'm noticing a change from the regular pattern of so-and-so's behavior..." or something much more objective and diplomatic. This way you sound like a professional, not expressing your subjective opinion but simply stating a fact.

7. Another thing on our list is "normal." The problem with this adjective is that it's very difficult to define and relate to. What does it mean nowadays? What type of business or what job is normal? What family model is normal? What

appearance, what car, what type of relationship or what kind of career is normal? In most situations, we can't objectively say that. Moreover, it's polarizing. When you say someone is normal, the other side of the coin is "not normal," which could be offensive to some people. Instead, it's much safer and smarter to say "average" or "usual." It's almost impossible to receive it wrong and misinterpret it, and it's much more specific, defined, and easier to relate to.

8. Now, the last one, and a little talk about the right attitude on top of that. In your utterances, you should change "Because..." to "Because I..." Let's say that you lost your job and it's hard to make a living now. You could say, "Because my boss fired me, I lost my job and now am struggling to make a living and..." or, "Because of the bad economy, I lost my job and now I'm..." Instead, you should say, "Because I used to spend too much and failed to save enough money to make a living before I'm able to find a new job or start a business..." or, "Because I stopped developing myself and learning new things, my boss was able to find people with higher qualifications than mine who would work for the same money..." Apart from the fact that you might really hate your boss and your bad situation might really also be caused by the bad economy, doing so trains your brain **not to shift responsibility to other people and circumstances** and makes you **learn from your own mistakes**, shortcomings and imperfections instead. Remember: changing your verbal patterns also changes your mental patterns. Next time, when someone asks you why you are late, instead of shifting the responsibility and asking for stupid excuses they are not likely to believe anyway, change the "Because my car engine stopped..." to "Because I forgot to take care of my car previously..." Simple and yet difficult. But definitely a powerful thing to start doing today!

Chapter 10: Verbal Dexterity

Language is a powerful instrument which gives us a lot of amazing opportunities. When used properly, it can lead your conversation wherever you want it to be, leave a great impression or influence your interlocutors' decisions.

In this chapter, you will learn about the patterns of linguistic dexterity, thanks to which you can easily change the way of thinking in most people. One of the most useful applications of these patterns is changing of people's beliefs.

I want to tell you about so-called "sleight of mouth," which was created by Robert Diltsa. He decided to analyze Richard Bandler's (the creator of NLP – Neuro-Linguistic Programming) most frequent patterns in his verbal communication. He picked the ones he found the most effective and modified them, creating his own system. Now "The Sleight of Mouth" is used by therapists and coaches all over the world, mainly as an effective instrument for changing beliefs in a conversation.

Long story short, it's a set of 14 language patterns, which you can use in practically every single conversation. These patterns are independent from each other and it's up to you to decide which will fit most in a particular situation.

Each pattern, in its own way, helps to extend the perspective and horizons of a person with whom you are talking and helps them notice more opportunities. Hereby, with some practice, you can change your interlocutors' beliefs quite easily.

It gives you the possibility to help others when they are trapped in their limited way of seeing the world. Once you learn to use these patterns, you will have the ability to persuade people that in addition to their limited perspective, there are also other, better options.

To make it easy for you to understand, I'm presenting all of the patterns as interpreted by me and slightly modified, with the example of three beliefs. You will now be able to empathize with contexts in which these techniques are most useful. At the end of this chapter, you will also find a few beliefs, which you can later work out by yourself.

Here are three detrimental beliefs, which we will be undermining by using the patterns:

a) It is difficult to learn languages!

b) NLP is not appropriate for our company.

c) It is hard to make new friends.

1. Hierarchy of Values

Connect a belief with some greater value.

a) Imagine the freedom and plethora of new possibilities the ability to speak foreign languages can give you!

b) Let's focus on how NLP can help you to succeed in the market and totally crush it in your niche.

c) A little bit of effort put in meeting new people will give you a lot of happiness and joy.

2. Intention

Change the intention of belief to a positive one.

a) That may also mean that the ability to learn new languages is very important and it is definitely worthwhile to gain it.

b) That's why it's the perfect opportunity for our company to finally open up to new ways of development.

c) It seems that this is the great opportunity to work on your own limits, and at the same time get to know some interesting and fun people.

3. Redefinition of Meaning

Change the meaning of the belief, using different words, which cause a different reaction.

a) The fact that someone had been learning Spanish for so long with mediocre results does not mean that everyone needs so much time and effort.

b) *It's not about NLP not getting along with the style and direction of our company. It's just that NLP must be properly and wisely implemented in order to bring great benefits.*

c) *It's not about how hard or easy meeting new people can be. Simply, it is worth it to put a little effort and attention into it, so the relationships we establish can be fulfilling for both sides and long-lasting.*

4. Consequences

Show a consequence which will undermine a belief.

a) *Will it be easier for you to never leave your country, or to go everywhere with a dictionary in your hand, mispronouncing the words constantly, butchering the language and making foreign stereotypes about our nation even stronger?*

b) *This approach will hold our employees back from getting the possibility of quick and effective development... and hence increased productivity and creativity.*

c) *The more difficult it is, the more it is worth to get to finally learn this ability... otherwise you can be alone for the rest of your life.*

5. Chunk Down

The descent to a more detailed level. Find one element of belief which will undermine it.

a) *The fact that different pronunciation is a problem for someone does not mean that you will also experience this.*

b) *I am totally convinced that the techniques of establishing good contact with clients can be very useful and profitable for us.*

c) *Exactly which element of meeting new people is specifically difficult for you?*

6. Chunk Up

Getting on a more general level. Generalize a belief, so you can see it from a different perspective.

a) Learning a new language always takes some time, but then you know it forever.

b) By saying this, do you mean to tell me that effective communication with clients is not appropriate for our company?

c) Remember that relationships with other people give true meaning and depth to our lives.

7. Counterexample

Find a concrete example which will undermine a belief.

a) For me, learning how to speak Spanish was extremely easy and fun.

b) I know this company with a similar profile to ours. They have been using NLP for a long time now and have had a lot of success.

c) Do you remember how you met John? It was totally natural for you and you understood each other very well from the very beginning!

8. Analogy

Use an analogy or a metaphor to undermine a belief.

a) I have a friend, according to whom everything is difficult. He hasn't achieved anything in his life yet.

b) I used to think that owning my own business was inappropriate for me. Now I run a very successful company.

c) In the same way as ants, building an anthill is hard work. Nevertheless, it is the meaning of their lives and that's how this species survived on this planet for hundreds of millions of years!

9. A Reference to Oneself

Refer the most important element of a belief and blame the person holding this belief.

a) ...and for me, it is hard to listen to another excuse like the one you're giving me.

b) I use NLP on a daily basis... does it mean that I'm inadequate for our company?

c) It's really me who it's hard for, when I have to beat that silly bullshit out of your head for another time.

10. A Different Result

Find another result of having that belief.

a) It is your life that's going to be hard if you're going to depend on other people all the time or act like a stereotypical dumb tourist abroad.

b) It is inappropriate to endanger our company by using outdated techniques which hardly work at all.

c) Your life will be hard when you find that you have nobody to turn to.

11. Change of Frame

Evaluate a belief by putting it in a different context.

a) If learning languages was really so difficult, there wouldn't be so many people speaking five or six different languages fluently, all language schools would be out of business and people would probably stop travelling anywhere on their own.

b) We should think how using NLP techniques in our company can change our course and raise our sales in a five-year perspective.

c) If what you said was true, everyone would be lonely and humans would have been extinct a long time ago.

12. Meta Frame

Formulate a belief about a belief.

a) I understand that you must know a lot about the learning process of many different languages of the world then?

b) Could it maybe be that NLP is not appropriate specifically for you, just because no one showed you how to apply it effectively?

c) So I assume that means you tried to meet all the people in the world already?

13. Model of the World

See a belief looking from a different perspective, from a point of view of a different model of the world.

a) You're probably just saying this to justify the fact that you haven't taken any action to learn a foreign language.

b) According to many famous and successful people, NLP is one of the best things that's ever happened to them.

c) The fact that this is such a big challenge makes it even more interesting and tempting.

14. Strategies of Reality

Make your interlocutor aware of the fact that a single belief may mean many various things, depending on a point of view.

a) What exactly do you mean by "hard"?

b) What exactly did you want to tell me by saying that "NLP is not appropriate"?

c) What does "hard" mean to you?

Now, when you are familiar with every pattern, you can start using it every time you talk to someone. The most important thing is to consciously pay attention to what the other person says. Listen carefully to everything they have to tell you and depending on a situation, use an appropriate language pattern. Some of these patterns and examples might be too cocky in some instances, whereas some of them might be too weak to pierce through someone's mind-shell. Sometimes you would have to be rather subtle (e.g. when talking to your teacher or professor), sometimes you would need to roll out the heaviest artillery to change the way someone thinks (I sometimes had to use several patterns to finally succeed in explaining something to someone). Deciding which of these patterns you should use is up to you, as every single case may be totally different and you have to take different circumstances into account.

You should especially pay attention to beliefs hidden in verbal messages, which say that someone is not able to do something, something is difficult or too hard, something is impossible, etc.

To make the ability of using these patterns more fluent, you should practice a lot. That's why it's best to choose two patterns per day and practice only those two. After some time, you should have really improved the ability to sense the context. That's when matching a pattern into a situation will come naturally. Your intuition itself will be giving you relevant things to say.

These patterns can be used practically everywhere: in negotiations, in a conversation with a client, in conversations with your partner, dispelling doubts in other people, motivating your loved ones, helping people to solve their problems. There are as many applications as topics of conversation.

Each day, select one or two patterns and practice. Pay attention to what happens when you use each of these patterns in a particular context.

Below, you can find another four beliefs, which can be broken down using verbal dexterity. Try to work them out by yourself:

 - *I can't start my own business because it's risky.*

 - *Relationships usually end in suffering.*

 - *Long walks are boring.*

 - *Only lucky people succeed in life.*

Start now!

Chapter 11: The Subtle Art of Giving Feedback

How can you effectively and politely tell people about their mistakes and shortcomings so that they start to work on themselves instead of getting bitter and demotivated? Feedback is an opinion which you give to the other person to let them know what to improve in their behavior or when performing a particular task.

Quite often, when we want to tell someone what they could improve or focus on, we get the effect opposite of the one desired—usually that person gets even more depressed (or pissed off) and does not think about taking our advice at all. How should we give feedback properly, so that the receiver can feel good and get a lots of motivation to improve their performance?

Imagine this situation: your friend is going to perform before a group of people and do a presentation on a certain topic. He stands in front of everyone and begins to talk. You sit at the audience, watching his speech and writing down the things that he does wrong and all the aspects he could improve on. His speech is not too good—he's holding his hands in his pockets, is not looking at his audience and is also talking too quickly. He ends the presentation and goes straight to you asking, "How was it?" You want him to perform much better next time, so you tell him what was wrong. "Well, you spoke a little too quickly, your gestures were chaotic and you closely examined all the walls in the room while you should have been looking at the group."

What is the outcome of such feedback? By commenting on his performance this way, **you only focus on his mistakes and provide him with a negative emotional content.** Your friend, getting a negative emotion, starts feeling bad and will probably not listen to your advice. He might even get depressed and be much more afraid or stressed out next time. On the other hand, you might be wondering why he behaves this way—after all, you are his friend and want the best for him.

So how do we go about giving feedback? Firstly, you need to be aware of the fact that **if you want someone to learn something, this person must be in a positive emotional state.** Motivation is a positive emotion. Even if you're motivated by bad things and prefer the so-called "negative motivation", the idea of motivation itself is still positive. If you only tell someone about their shortcomings and provide them with negative emotions, in most cases you will only demotivate them. People are not able to learn effectively when they feel bad. The key here is to associate the feedback containing information about what should be done differently with positive emotions.

Sandwich Feedback

Sandwich feedback is a model of giving feedback, which allows us to motivate people instead of giving those negative feelings. If you have ever watched the TV show *Shark Tank* this is how (usually, sometimes it gets brutal) "the Sharks" give feedback to people before or after rejecting their deals. This model consists of three stages:

1. **A positive emotion.** At the beginning of giving feedback, you must show the person you give it to that they did well. You can say, "This is what should have been done, congrats"; "Good job, you did great!"; "A great performance". If this person's performance was obviously poor, then of course you will not say, "Wow! What a revelation!", because they will simply think are making fun of them. In that case, you can just say: "Good job, congrats on your first try!"
   After the initial approval, tell them about two or three things that they've done well. Provide specific examples! You can say, "You really knew the topic well!" Or, "It's great that you spoke loud enough!" Appreciate their effort. It is about making them feel great at the start. Joy and relaxation are states conducive for learning and motivation.

2. **What to improve?** On the second stage, you tell them all those things they did wrong, but in a positive overtone. So, you do not say what they did wrong but **what can they do better.** You do not say: "You were talking too fast!", but rather, "You could have spoken a little bit more slowly; the audience would have understood you much better then." Instead of, "You were ill-mannered," you should say, "You could have been a little more polite," and so on. Additionally, you can already give that person the solution for their particular problem.
   For example, if a friend of yours has problems with establishing contacts with new people and he has just spoken to someone, you can tell him exactly what to do. "Listen, man, what you really need to get along with people better is to put

a smile on your face from time to time. You need more openness—look them in the eyes more often and listen carefully to what they have to say." Just a short comment about what the person has to do better may not be enough. If you have adequate knowledge, it is worth it to say immediately exactly what that person should do to solve the problem, so next time this error won't occur.

3. **Positive emotion.** You end the conversation by evoking joy and relaxation again. You could say, "Well, like I said though, generally you did great!" At the end, you need a little praise again.

Based on the example I gave you earlier, how would the situation from the beginning of the chapter look? Using a sandwich feedback, this is what you could say to your friend who just performed his first public speech: "Not bad, it was a really nice presentation. I liked how you told this joke; everyone liked it. I see that you have a lot of knowledge on this topic. Among some things that you could have done better is certainly your speaking rate—I would advise you to speak more slowly. Before you start speaking, take a few deep breaths, it will relax you and enable you to slow down a little bit. Also, remember to look people in the eyes. They will be able to feel that you're talking directly to them. Additionally, you could work on hand gestures a little bit. Recently I read a great book about body language. I will bring it to you tomorrow. In general, though, this was a great performance. Congratulations!"

How do you think this message would be received by your friend? What would be his attitude after he hears these words? Would he be depressed or would he more likely say, "Wow, cool! I will try to improve these things! Thanks!" Another way of communication with a completely different effect.

It may be not the reflection of the harshest truth, but instead, you give people a wonderful gift in the form of constructive feedback, and lots of motivation so they can start applying the advice immediately and hence the opportunity to become better in what they do. As a result, instead of depression and the absence of desire for development, you will see a wild desire for improvement.

The so-called "sandwich feedback" can be used in many different contexts. If you are a student, you can use it to motivate and teach your friends who have problems with their upcoming exams. You can advise people how to give better public speeches or play better concerts. If you are a parent, you can use it to motivate your children without making them feel bad and overly pressured. It can bring excellent educational effects when used properly on kids. As a teacher, you can use sandwich feedback to motivate your students. As a CEO or a manager, you can tell your employees what they need to improve without upsetting and annoying them, so you don't feel hostility in your own office. As a son, daughter, brother or sister, you can help your family and friends in many different ways. Now, think about real life situations in which you can use this knowledge, and apply it as soon as possible!

What's also worth mentioning in the context of giving feedback is delivering difficult messages when we want to ask people to change their behavior. Often when we want to tell people something important, we take for granted that, for example, "This worker's position in this company is solid," or that, "Our relationship is great." However, the other party may not know that. Has your boss ever asked you to talk for a moment, and you knew they wanted to tell you something important, so your self-talk started going louder and louder? "What's wrong? What does he want to tell me? Am I getting fired?" Then, after five minutes the boss told you that you shouldn't leave the office half an hour earlier and you should do something else instead and call someone, you say to yourself, "Ooooh! Am I not fired? What a relief... Ok... Wait... What did he say?" If you want people to really listen to you and avoid causing bad emotions in them which may lead to unwanted behaviors, it's crucial to address whatever fear they might have at the beginning of the conversation. So, for example, when speaking to your employee you could say, "Bob, you know that you are a great employee and that you have a great future with us; however, I just wanted to ask you to..." Or, for instance: "Honey, you know I love you and I see my entire future with you, but I would really appreciate if you could you please stop..." This way you are slowing down their self-talk and calming their emotions. Do this whenever you think someone might have even the slightest doubts about your relation with them, or about some kind of situation that may end, etc. It will save you lot of time and energy. It's also a very classy thing to do.

Another great thing you can do when you want to start a difficult conversation with someone and to make people drop their guard a little bit is to ask them to help you with a task. For example, if you want to talk about something rather difficult with your kids, you could ask them to help you prepare a salad or some other dish, or maybe pay them to help you paint the fence to make them focus on the work even more. That way you are lowering their defense, making them listen more carefully and intuitively as they're focused on a particular task and it's much easier to even start the conversation without creating unnecessary tension. You should also remove as many distractions like smartphones, computer, TV, etc. as possible. You can also use it at work, asking your employee or co-worker to help you with organizing files, moving boxes, etc. It's much better idea than just saying, "Hey, Daniel, see me in my office in five minutes." Try it and you will be surprised how effective it can be.

Last thing I want to tell you in this chapter is how to deal well with negative feedback and criticism. When somebody is criticizing your work and giving you negative feedback, you need to remember that what you are doing physically also affects what is going on mentally. When people criticize us, we often tend to close down our body language. At the same time, the ability to receive negative feedback is something very valuable and useful in life and appreciated in many companies.

The first thing you need to do is to raise your head, straighten your spine, put your shoulders back and open your chest. You need to physically be open to receive that message, which will help you receive the criticism mentally. It's not easy, but very necessary and helpful, a skill you can and you should learn. The very next thing you should do is to relate to the negative feedback. Let's say your boss told you, "Your work report is too short and I don't like the way you worded it. I can't accept it in its current form." You could say, "OK, so the problem is that it's too short and my wording should be better..." Here you need to repeat the criticism back to the person. At the end, you need to ask a solution oriented question. For example, you could ask, "If I write an extra two thousand words and rephrase it, will you be able to accept it?" You could also try a different approach and ask, "Alright, if I could show you evidence to support my belief that my work report is long enough and straight to the point, that it doesn't require much time for our employees to read, and the language I used will be easy for them to understand, would you be then willing to accept it?" So, let's recap: you need to open your body language, then make sure you understood what was said correctly and finally, specify the steps to resolve the problem. If you train yourself in doing so, you will be perceived as a much more effective, experienced and professional communicator.

Chapter 12: How to Become a Master of the Sharp Retort

Everyone knows the feeling of finding only emptiness in your head at the exact moment that what you need most is a retort that's sharp like a razor, perfectly matched to the context. It's one of those things you definitely don't want to happen often, yet it keeps coming back during the most unexpected situations. Wouldn't it be great to always have smart, sharp and funny retorts at your hand, everywhere and anytime you want them?

It's high time to master the art of responding with witty retorts to any unpleasant comments and annoying remarks aimed at you. Below, you will find **10 ways to train a sharp tongue** that will surprise your friends, parents, colleagues from work, strangers on the street and even your dog.

You probably know the annoying feeling when you keep coming back to a past situation, imagining what you could have said, and how the annoying person would look if you had this or that great response in your mind back then... These are usually the moments when you've already managed to calm yourself down and have had a while to rethink things. That's when suddenly, the best retorts come to mind, but "If I only said that!" doesn't change anything as it's already too late.

To annihilate this problem, you need to learn things that will fill your head with hundreds of retorts for any given occasion.

The art of the retort is very subtle. Not only is it about knowing what to say in a particular moment, but also it needs to be done and said in the right way. It is not enough to know only the techniques that can help you find a great retort. You need a foundation, the right approach to what other people say.

A mix of all these elements creates a special skill that allows you to have your guard raised all the time without any effort from your side.

Granted, I won't give you any prewritten texts or so-called "canned material" here. Learning someone else's retorts by heart would be the best recipe for making you someone as close to sharp retorts as politicians are to telling the truth. Believe me, such an approach would make you miss that perfect moment to shoot your verbal bullet as each single time you would wonder, "Which response should I use?" for too long.

Instead of that, in this chapter I will tell you about spontaneity—the key to make your answers natural, different and unique each single time. So if you are ready and want to become a master of the witty retort, get to know each of the points below and start to work!

1. First and foremost—distance yourself from your own flaws and what other people say about you and simply chill out! Even if these are unpleasant comments concerning your weak points, people often do this out of fear, or because they do not feel secure in your company. Some people do it to raise their own status when they feel inferior. If you took everything others people say personally, you would constantly go into negative emotional states, which block your creativity and skill of choosing perfect words.

When you distance yourself, you do not care what other people say and you are able to quickly and coherently respond to someone else's words. Remember, whatever people say, they are **only words**! For the most part people do not mean what they say and do it only for the purposes listed above. Accept this fact as well as your flaws, and no one will be able to make you feel unpleasant emotions without your permission.

2. Instead of taking things personally, you need relaxation, calmness and peace—that's the only state of mind where sharp retorts come naturally. Moreover, the mere act of responding to someone in a nervous way disqualifies your retort and does not allow it to get on the podium. Imagine a stressful person, who stuttering and sweating tries to stammer a droll retort! It would not pass and just ridicule the poor guy. Say what you have to say with relaxation and peace, and certainly it will sound as it should.

3. Look serious while giving a retort. Do not laugh while speaking. When you're serious, it increases the effect and makes everyone around even more amused. Note that jokes told in a serious tone are usually way funnier than those told by a laughing person. Do some acting and throw your retort suddenly, with a deadly seriousness. Of course, this rule has its exceptions, as you will read in following paragraphs.

4. A good retort usually goes outside the box in which a message preceding the retort is set. It is supposed to be something surprising, something the other person will not be expecting. Many times you have probably witnessed an explosion of laughter right after someone aptly replied with a good retort. Such volleys of laughter mostly appear after something totally unexpected.

5. Relate to the most popular current topic or trend. All you need in order to do this is the most basic knowledge about events occurring in the world and in our country. There is no shortage of scandals and strange or funny events in our homeland, so you can always tell a retort connected with a situation in which one of the politicians or celebrities offended someone after they felt dishonored, etc... There are many options, if you watch the news at least sometimes (I wouldn't really recommend watching mainstream news too often!) or you sometimes follow these things online, then it's easy to refer to what's currently on most people's minds as soon as the opportunity arises.

6. Use reframing. It is one of the best NLP techniques and comes down to seeing the same thing from a completely new perspective. There are two types of reframing: content and context reframing. In content reframing, if you want to find a good answer, you need to you ask yourself the question: "What different, positive meaning could this particular situation have?" In context reframing, you need to answer this question: "In what other context would this situation would seem positive?"

7. "This is my favorite story!" Sometimes you meet people who talk too much— they start talking about what you did wrong or how you should behave, and you cannot see the end of their criticism. At this point you can interject their monologue, preferably at the very beginning of it: "Oh yes, I love this story!" This strategy requires you to say it with a smile and joy in your eyes, as if you really enjoy what you are going to hear. It will knock your critic off guard. It is very useful when you are in a bigger group (at least a few people), because then you can turn to others by saying, "Listen to this carefully; it is really great!" It often applies lots of pressure on your critics and gets them off track.

8. "Speaking of shoelaces..." If your interlocutor started talking about something you don't want to mention or discuss, you can suddenly and surprisingly change the subject to something entirely different. Change it to one that has something to do with the issue this person wanted to bring up, however, lead the conversation in a completely different direction. Imagine that someone says to you, "Your shoes do not fit the trousers you are wearing," and you say, "Speaking about shoelaces, have you heard of the world's longest shoelace, according to the Guinness Records book?" Or less neutral: "Speaking of shoes, do you think that if I lubricated your bald head with a black shoe polish, it would shine bright like a diamond?"

9. Amuse yourself and others. Remember to use clever retorts in order to lower the tension, to make yourself and others laugh or simply to improve the atmosphere. It is not worth doing it in an impolite or rude manner as it will just generate unnecessary conflicts which can then escalate into something worse. Whenever there is a risk that your words will ignite an argument, then the best retort is usually just silence or ignoring of the other person. The real master of the sharp retort is a person who knows when to stop the discussion, even with the retort of the year (or even of the century) on their minds. I know that sometimes it's hard to stop yourself when something really funny and accurate wants to escape your lips, but believe me—there are moments when it is better to swallow some words and keep them for a better occasion.

Try to use this ability only when you know that the other person will take it with a smile or at least with a positive attitude. Enjoy it, entertain others with it, unleash your creativity and surprise everyone around you, but use it for a good cause.

10. Take away these "magic bullets": At the beginning of this chapter, I told you I won't be giving you any ready retorts and "canned material", but this will serve as a good exception. With these phrases you can respond to anything anybody ever tells to you when buying yourself time to think and regain composure.

The phrases always start with, "That's interesting," and they are:

"That's interesting. Why would you say that?"

"That's interesting. Why would you do that?"

"That's interesting. Tell me more."

"That's interesting. Why would you ask that?"

There's nothing that you can't respond to using these phrases.

Moreover, they also get people off track and make them realize how stupid, futile or vain the things they tell you are. Also, they sometimes have the power to make your interlocutors start thinking really deeply about their real motives and the intentions behind what they told you and what they threw at you, and simply surrender or suddenly change their attitude to a much nicer one. They sometimes work as a "wake up slap."

11. Practice with yourself. Your internal dialogue, constantly commenting on the surrounding reality, can be very useful. Just sit for a few minutes in a quiet and peaceful place and start talking with your own mind. It can be done out loud, but if you do not want your family to take you to a psychiatric ward you'd better choose to practice only in your mind. You will need two inner voices: one should be your friend's, and the other your own.

The exercise is very simple—you need to imagine this person saying to you some unpleasant, mean or insulting things. Then you think of some good, relevant, creative retort. Of course, in the beginning, coming up with such retorts can take a few minutes or longer, but having dialogues with your own mind shouldn't be so strange, since almost everyone on this planet is doing it on a daily basis. No matter how much time it takes you at first, you will become better with practice. Once you come up with a juicy retort, let your inner voice tell you something unpleasant again. You'll see that in a short time, good answers will appear faster and faster. Practice it as often as possible!

Once you master the above points, you will become a conjurer who juggles with words. Retorts as sharp as a Japanese katana blade will be flowing out from your mouth just when the situation requires it. Work on improving your ability to find relevant answers and you will see that in some time it will be completely natural for you. Have fun and good luck!

Chapter 13: How to Have Unique and Memorable Conversations

How often do you have conversations which you can describe as fascinating or really witty? Do you frequently talk with other people in a way which feeds your soul, makes your mind tingle pleasantly and leaves you fully content? Even a usual chit-chat can be a memorable experience.

In this chapter I will show you ways of taking your communication skills to a more advanced level. Thanks to these cool tricks, you will be able to make every conversation unique, whether it will be an informal conversation, a negotiation or business conversations.

Some time ago I went to this interesting seminar about emotional intelligence. During one of the lunch breaks, I had a brief conversation with another participant of the training. The guy was several years older than me. I had no opportunity to get to know him better until then and frankly, I expected this conversation to be typical and a little bit boring small talk.

You rarely can be SO wrong. Just at the very beginning of exchanging our opinions it struck me that it clearly wouldn't be another usual obvious small talk between two strangers. Everything we discussed somehow concerned the most important things to me back in the day, and I was challenged to think very differently and look at the whole thing from an entirely new perspective. More than once I had to take a moment to reflect on my response to be able to reach an important and meaningful conclusion. The real solid workout for my mind intertwined with frequent explosions of laughter made this conversation stay in my memory for a very long time.

Since that day I would often wonder why some conversations are just usual chit-chat fluff-type time fillers, while others can be a unique, almost spiritual experience. By doing a conscious observation while carefully listening to conversations of others and testing of various different concepts, I came to sudden realization that how any particular conversation goes depends vastly on myself.

I can give it a tone, change its direction, fascinate an interlocutor or invite them to answer interesting, challenging and tricky questions. I can do a whole bunch of things, becoming a source of fascinating conversation. And what is the most interesting, it does not only apply to chats with friends—imagine how powerful and useful it can be in business or in negotiations!

In this chapter I will show you the **eleven most useful ideas to make a conversation unique.** They are all briefly described below with examples and links to wider sources of knowledge on a particular subject. Learn, test and check the effects!

1. Use the Matrix of Entry

By a good conversation starter, you can define the way in which it will be received. If you start with, "Dude, yesterday something absolutely amazing happened to me," then the entire content of what you say will be received by the listener as something extraordinary. If instead of this you say, "Man, yesterday something extremely instructive happened to me," then the same content would be received as more instructive than incredible.

How can you benefit from knowing about this? Say to someone, "I have really cool proposition for you!" or, "Focus, because what I tell you in a moment will really give you food for thought." There is a whole bunch of opportunities! Remember, a matrix of entry is something you always use in the very beginning of a conversation, or whenever subject of the conversation changes or is just about to change. Thanks to this simple fix you always have the certainty that your message will be received the way you defined it. You simply put it in a good frame.

2. Tell Stories and Use Metaphors

Not only are analogies a great tool in psycho-therapies, they also prove very useful in everyday conversations. An accurate story or metaphor is like a skeleton key to the mind of the other person. It will be enough if you think about what situation from your life is similar to the event which you and your interlocutor were just talking about.

Then you just say "It reminds me of a similar story..." or "It is just as if it..." and you continue. It should usually fascinate your interlocutors and stimulate their imagination.

3. Discover Your Interlocutors' Beliefs and Values

Find out what is important to this person and what they think about the world around them. It can be easily observed during first several minutes of the talk, especially on some more serious life-related topics, when the other person starts expressing their opinions, beliefs, life philosophy and their view on crucial things like relationships, health, money, career, education, religion, politics (although that's a topic you should really avoid in your conversations), family, sports, et cetera. On the foundation of this crucial knowledge you can build a rapport, showing your interlocutor that you also have a similar view (but this is not an entirely necessary step, especially when your view is totally different—it would most probably appear fake). It is enough to just direct the conversation to topics that are important to this person and that's it. **Everyone likes to talk about the important things in their lives. If you can change the track of the conversation so you talk about topics important and interesting both to you and your interlocutor, you hit the bullseye.** It's usually possible, even if the person you're talking with lives by different values, on a different level of social ladder, is much younger or older, etc. By showing interest in these topics, you will surely cause this person to really involve themselves in the conversation and immerse in it much more deeply.

4. Get to Know Your Interlocutor's Metaprograms

Metaprograms are individual filters of thinking. When you know more precisely how the person with whom you have a conversation thinks, you are able to use this knowledge very effectively, for example **to motivate or strongly inspire them to do something (or restrain from something). You will have a chance to learn more about this topic in the chapter called "Metaprograms."**

5. Enjoy and Use Your Own Voice

Do not let it be monotonous and colorless, because this is the fastest way to make your interlocutor fall asleep. You need to modulate your voice and make it engaging. Sometimes speak loudly, then go quieter. Sometimes slowly, sometimes more rapidly. Use stops, which evoke the feeling of strong curiosity and mystery. Change your intonation. You can sometimes (don't overdo it) imitate voices of people you are talking about if it's not offensive, or do impressions of characters from movies and cartoons to make people laugh (unless you have zero stand-up and acting skills, in that case hold off until you train them a little). Keep practicing and listening to your voice and soon it will be a pure pleasure for everyone to listen to you talk. Since you can't actually hear the real sound of your voice, it is a very good idea to record your monologues from time to time or to join a Toastmasters club or some other public speaking or acting classes. There are lots of these activities you can find and join on sites like meetup.com and many different places online. Don't think twice, **these skillsets are really useful in everyday life, business and your career** and you will also probably meet lots of great people.

6. Ask Penetrating Questions about the Topic

You can lead entire conversations only by asking good questions (which, by the way, is a great mind exercise) on which you can learn much more about the topic and your speaker. When your interlocutor stops talking, ask them any question regarding the content of their speech. When they are responding, **listen carefully and actively to what they are saying**—they will feel your involvement (even though you will be silent) and will appreciate it. People love when someone really listens to them and they love talking about themselves!

7. Ask Unique Questions

Unique questions distinguish your conversation from the grey crowd, stimulate your speaker's imagination and really make you think. Some examples: "If you had a passive fixed income of 40,000 USD provided every single month, what would you do with your life? Which dreams would you fulfill?"; "What do you want your life to look like three years from now?"; "What was the best day of your life?"; "What makes you laugh the most?"; "If there were no limits, what would you want to do in five minutes?" and so on. There are infinite amounts of such questions—it all comes down to your creativity. Sometimes a single question like that can be enough to build an extremely interesting conversation.

8. Induce Feelings

Tap into all kinds of emotions! Make sure that there is laughter, joy, occasional tension and uncertainty, and at other times curiosity, mystery and fascination in your conversations. You can also use the so-called "emotional rollercoaster"—tell your interlocutors about something very cheerful, then about something rather sad to break the emotional state (but don't overdo it, you don't want your interlocutors depressed or crying), and then again about something very uplifting, relaxing and joyful. Strong **emotions engage people in a conversation and get both sides in the state of flow**—instead of thinking about what to say, you just speak. You do not simply talk to each other, but you are having a real conversation where both sides are fully engaged and present in the moment. You don't want to overuse this technique and do it every single time you talk to a person, but it is especially helpful at the beginning, when you get to meet someone or want to be remembered.

How do you induce emotions? The best idea is to feel them yourself. If you want to make the other person feel curious, first feel it yourself, then start telling them about something with great curiosity. The so-called mirror neurons[7] ensure that they will quickly start feeling very similar emotions to these you are feeling at the moment[8].

9. Lead Conversations

Are you bored with talking about the same thing for too long? Do you have a much more interesting idea in your mind? With a little bit of ingenuity and you can lead conversations in the direction you want them to go. **The only thing you have to do**

---

[7] http://www.scholarpedia.org/article/Mirror_neurons
[8] http://www.kuleuven.be/mirrorneuronsystem/readinglist/Rizzolatti%20&%20Craighero%202004%20-%20The%20MNS%20-%20ARN.pdf

is to "catch" particular parts of your interlocutor's speech and start a new thread on this previous foundation. For example, when someone talks about how last year they were in the hospital for two weeks and how awful it was, you can interject with: "One month ago I was also unlucky enough to visit the hospital for an extended period of time. I spent almost all that time watching movies on my laptop. Have you watched any interesting movies lately?" When someone is complaining all the time about how bad the situation in our country is and you don't feel like listening to it for fifth time in a row, you can say, "Well, you're right, our government could work more efficiently. But that doesn't change the fact that our country is extremely beautiful—I went to the mountains recently and you won't believe what happened to me..."

Another example: imagine that while negotiating, your interlocutor pays too much attention to the high price of your product. You could say: "The price is totally adequate to the premium quality of the product. We are the best in terms of quality, please pay attention to the exotic materials this product is made of..." At the beginning, such actions can seem difficult to you, but as soon as you get the general idea, it becomes pretty simple. With a little practice you can change the subjects of conversation as often as you like.

10. Finish the Conversation at the Perfect Moment

It is no art to totally drain a topic and finish the conversation when there is nothing more to say, as it makes you end up in an undesired emotional state. End when there is still some hunger, curiosity or any other good emotion. This feeling should remain in your interlocutor's memory for some time after you finish your conversation and thus they will still be thinking about the nice talk you had. Moreover, it will probably make them come back for more in order to satisfy this hunger.

11. Build a Good Rapport

Lastly and most importantly, by matching both non-verbal (body language, voice, and breathing) and verbal (experiences, beliefs, and values) aspects of communication you can build a unique atmosphere of trust during every conversation. **After making a**

good match you can start to lead—causing that the other person to follow the direction in which you point.

A good rapport will make using each of these methods for having a unique conversation much more simple. Once you learn how to use all of the above ways in your conversations, you will be surprised with the great results you'll get. In fact, there is no need to master every single one of these ideas, just a few that you like the most are enough to raise the quality of most of your interactions.

Be sure to learn it step-by-step. If you try to learn all of these ideas at once, it won't work. Choose one method per day and practice it during every conversation. Thanks to this, you will develop new habits of effective communication, which will stay with you for a long time.

Chapter 14: Rapport, the Art of Excellent Communication

Do you want to know the key to absolutely effective communication? Would you like to learn how to establish the subtle thread of understanding with other people really fast? Thanks to good rapport, you will be able to create an atmosphere of trust, cooperation and mutual understanding which will make the people with whom you communicate familiar, safe and at ease. Knowledge which you will now acquire will give you the ability to evoke in your interlocutors the impression that you both "transmit on the same wavelength." The truth is that **we like people who are similar to us** and it is them who we trust the most.

Think for a moment, who do you like to spend your time with the most? Do these people have similar views, beliefs and interests who speak and behave in a similar way to you? Of course, this is not a rule, but this is who you usually feel the best with.

Not only is the ability to quickly establish such a deep connection and understanding crucial in interpersonal relations, but also in business, therapy or sales. In this chapter I will exactly explain to you what the "rapport" thing is and how to create that bridge to a better understanding to make others feel comfortable with us, to make them trust us and also open up a little bit more. Thanks to this, you give both them and yourself a chance to create a strong relationship in a much shorter time.

Building the atmosphere of trust and mutual understanding is the most effective way quickly establish a solid relationship between two interlocutors. In this chapter, you will learn the basics of so-called "mirroring" as well as what "leading" is.

Since nonverbal communication (mainly body language and our voice) is a big part of the entire communication process, we can usually tell if communication between two people occurs harmoniously or clumsily and chaotically, even if they speak the Martian language.

Let me begin with an example:

Imagine a couple sitting at a table.

He sits laid back and relaxed. Seated on the chair, his legs are extended and straight. Hands in pockets, breathing quietly. Speaks slowly and softly.

She is much more nervous looking. Sitting hunched, tense muscles can be seen. Legs bent and crossed. Clenched fists on the table. She speaks loudly and quickly; you can hear the anger.

How do you think these two people get along? Is there an understanding and cooperation between them?

Now imagine another pair. Seated at a table, both in the same position. Their arms are on the table and they're holding hands. They look at each other with a similar expression. They both speak in a very similar way: slowly, clearly and warmly. Do they feel comfortable? Is there more harmony and trust and less stress between them?

Considering these two cases, we know that the body language of these people works unconsciously. It adapts to the relationships that exist between these two people. NLP says that you can control those factors consciously. This way you can change your body language and the tone of your voice to create understanding and establish meaningful contact with the other person. You can adjust to a person's gestures and manner of speaking to gain trust and begin to create a strong bond. This skill is extremely useful in virtually every area of life in which you contact other people.

In other words, rapport is a skill of matching body language and tone of voice with the person you are communicating with. To some extent it's about miming your interlocutor's behavior. Let me remind you that this is not meant to be a typical imitation though, about which you will read later. In psychology such behavior is called "mirroring". The goal is to create harmony and synchronization, through which you can build an effective and deep understanding.

How to Create Rapport?

Let me now show you the areas in which you can become more like the person you are talking to. Change your posture so that it is similar to the attitude of the other person. Here is what exactly you can adjust:

Body Language

- The general posture. Closed or open, the body curled or spread out and relaxed. If someone is lying on their back, do the same. Adjust arms and legs, but also direction you are facing when sitting, etc.

- Gestures. **You do not want to do exactly the same gestures.** You should do it differently, but just as energetically or as quietly. Adjust them elegantly and gracefully and remember that it has to be very subtle and unnoticed.

- Facial expression. If the person you are talking to is sad, do not smile all the time. You don't need to have the same expression though—it should just reflect the same set of emotions.

- Eye contact. When someone avoids your eyes and looks at you for brief moments, do not stare at them. The person will feel better when you give them some space and also reduce your eye contact. Also, another very important thing to remember is that we have been programmed over thousands of years to subconsciously perceive prolonged eye-contact as sign of aggression. So remember—eye contact is good, but too much eye contact is bad. You should never look people in eyes for more than 7 seconds nonstop. It's a typical communication-newbie mistake, kind of a creepy thing to do, even though we've been conditioned to look people in the eyes in our Western culture. Also, remember not to open your eyes too wide (the same thing, sign of aggression...or psychosis).

Voice

- Speech rate. Imagine a man who always speaks very quickly and clearly who has a meeting with a girl who speaks very slowly. Do you think it will be easy for them to bond?

- Gaps in speech. If your conversation partner makes a clear break between words or sentences, speak to them in a similar way. Omitting the pauses would hold back that person from understanding your message.

- Tone of your voice. Learn how to modulate your voice tone and start fitting it with the tone of the person you're speaking with.

Emotions

A very important point. Many people make the mistake of being happy and smiling when they want to comfort the other person. It brings a completely opposite effect—your cheerful consolation might upset the person even more. If you want to comfort them, try to understand the problem and show your sympathy. Adjust your emotions, and it will make that person feel better. Only after the creation of deep rapport can you begin to slowly change your attitude to a more joyful one and lead the person to a better well-being.

Breath

The pace and depth of breathing. Matching breathing can sometimes be a really strong incentive to create a rapid and profound rapport. How to see the other person's breath? Follow their nose, chest or arms. You will see how quickly and how deeply their breathing is.

Words

Some people use specific words in their statements such as: just, exactly, likewise, etc. Using these words from time to time when talking to them could be very useful.

On a verbal level, you can create rapport by matching:

- **Interlocutor's experiences.** In the communication process, the exchange of experiences plays a huge role and you can use that to your advantage. When your partner tells you about various events and experiences of their life, always think how you can relate those experiences to your own life. It does not have to be exactly the same experience; sometimes it is sufficient that one part is a little similar. If you can find such a situation in your life, share it with the person. An example in which experiences are not identical may be a situation where someone tells you how they broke their arm riding a bike. If you ever have broken a finger playing basketball, it is a great time to mention it. I often use it when I have an individual coaching session with someone. When, for example, my client starts telling me how much he is tormented by his internal dialogues which do not allow him to fall asleep, I will surely mention that I had a similar problem some time ago and that I managed to solve it. So he knows that I experienced the same and that I can help him.

Matching experiences is a very strong element of the rapport, because it creates the impression that two people have a similar, or even common past.

- **Beliefs and values.** When you talk to someone, try noticing what kind of values this person is guided by. Try to determine what the most important thing to them is. For example, if health holds the first place in their value system, you can mention, "Health is extremely important indeed, because it enables us to enjoy everything else we are given in our lives," etc. Very simple yet effective. Where else can you use it? Before you go to a work interview, you can check the interviewer's profiles on social media. Is your boss-to-be a religious person? You can mention about how you travelled around South America and was in awe of people being not ashamed to show their devotion and how proud of it you were. Believe me, it works just great (field tested).

Your conversation partner's beliefs are nested in the deep structures of the brain and their reflection has an immediate effect on the physiology of the person with whom you are communicating. Beliefs are shown when someone's speech starts from expressions such as: "I believe that...," "It seems to me that...," "I'm sure...," and not only because opinions and views on the surrounding reality are expressed in very different ways. It is important to know what that person thinks about the topic.

Reaffirming your callers' maps helps them open up to you, which is the key to establishing lasting relationships. When you talk with an acquaintance and you find out that, for example, they believe social actions like helping children from orphanages is something worth spending money on, you can show them that you have a similar belief.

This is, of course, not about agreeing with everyone all the time. An exchange of totally different beliefs may be a beginning of a great discussion. Use this tool whenever you'll find it useful though.

- **Characteristic expressions.** People often have regularly repeating words and phrases in their linguistic repertoire. This is related to the way in which mind encodes information. These formulations might be, for example: "in fact," "just," "exactly" or "absolutely."

Catching up on such expressions and using them from time to time will give your interlocutor's subconscious a signal that you speak their language. Just remember not to overdo it—then a conscious part of that person's mind will become aware of it and your interlocutor might think that you making fun of them.

- **Characteristic words relating to specific senses**. While communicating, we use words and phrases such as, "It is clear to me," "I feel it," or "It sounds great." All of these expressions have a similar meaning. However, they represent a different sense. The first is the sense of sight, the second - feeling, the third - hearing.

When most people speak, they often **predominantly use one of them.** When at the particular moment they are more visual in their talking, you will find words like: "clear," "simple," "I can see," "a perspective." In the case of a person using more of a sense of feeling, there may be words like: "I feel," "hard," "hold," "smoothly," "touch," etc.

When it comes to sensory perceptions, there are three main types that you can gather from a person depending on the way the person uses language to communicate with others:

- Visual – People whose sensory perception is visual would tend to use "seeing" phrases such as "my vision is clear," "I see what you mean," "your future is bright," and words such as "view," "imagine," "color," "hazy," "clear," "foresee," "appear," or "outlook." They also tend to describe things in terms of "seeing" such as "small," "light," "brown," "rectangular," etc.

- Auditory – People whose sensory perception is auditory would tend to use "hearing" phrases such as "I hear you," "she scratched the floor," "his voice was sharp," "I am listening to you," and words such as "listen," "talk," "discuss," "hear," "sound," "call," etc. They also tend to describe form in terms of "hearing" such as "loud," "noisy," "beeping," "ticking," etc.

- Kinesthetic – People whose sensory perception is kinesthetic tend to use "feeling" phrases such as "I feel that is the best way to do it," "My feelings do not support this," "She was warmly welcoming," "I feel that," "I can't grasp that" or "I fear that," and words such as "touch," "feel," "afraid," "fear," "warm," "cool," "rough," "smooth," "wet," etc.

Pay attention to these details and learn to adjust your style of speaking accordingly. First, you can practice creating longer sentences having a characteristic of each type of sensory perception above, so it becomes easy and natural for you to use them during real conversations. Pick one of those rapport-building techniques and use it in your next conversation. Then try another one and test how it works for you.

Every time focus on just one element, **teaching your brain what exactly it should catch in the other person's speaking.** Thanks to this, you will learn the ability step-by-step and will soon be able to use it automatically. Then, being able to adjust yourself through all of these ways at once, you will become a significantly better communicator.

I will also tell you about different, often repeating, verbal patterns and models of thinking and how to recognize them and utilize this knowledge. We'll also talk about other aspects of verbal rapport in the chapters "Metaprograms" and "Meta Model."

It is important that you remember to be vigilant and careful when you talk and listen to people. Besides the fact that I promised myself to carefully listen to other people's words long time ago, I would often find myself in a situation when at some point I forgot to pay attention to the linguistic structure and turned the "autopilot" on instead, losing track of my goal in the conversation.

With time, however, I developed the ability to be present and attentive to what the other person was saying. I started noticing the beliefs and values, experiences, specific words and phrases relating to the senses very easily. Remember, it's just another skill that you can learn.

This knowledge gives you great opportunities. Use it effectively and start to use it in your life as soon as you can.

The Most Important Things to Remember while Building Rapport!

1. Creating a rapport with the other person does not have to rely on miming everything that person is doing. **It is not, in any event, about typical imitation, overacting and copying everything.** The secret lies in the fact that your actions are subtle and unobtrusive.

2. The adjustment will be discreet if you do not do it violently. Do it slowly, being careful step by step. Do it so that it is invisible to the other person. Initial matching may take 2 minutes or more.

3. You do not need to match everything (and you really shouldn't). Start by observing and noticing what the most visible characteristic of the person is, and then select the specifics that you can match easily.

4. If there is a risk that the harmonization of one element would be too visible, you cannot do this directly. For example, nervous movements of the hand of another person may be reflected by rocking your body. Quick speaking can be reflected with a fast movement of your hand.

5. Remember that to have a good fit, you need to notice all the nonverbal signals of the other people first. So before you start to create a rapport, observe. Learn to notice the different elements of human behavior and practice this observation every time.

6. Observe your caller's reactions. See if they feel more comfortable thanks to your actions. The signals may be different—relaxation, smiling, opening up to your propositions, visible better mood, increased understanding of your messages, etc. Since everybody is different, you will have to remain flexible and alert. Never take anything for granted when building rapport.

7. Rapport can be also applied to any other part of communication with others. The point being you should also try to speak your interlocutor's language. We all have different symbolic language that we speak in all areas of our lives. For example, let's

take appreciation under our magnifier. Imagine that your colleague from work wanted to say "thank you" for your help with his project and gave you a bottle of premium bourbon or red wine. If someone said "thank you" to me this way, I would be really happy, but my cousin, for example, would be a little bit unfulfilled because his language is spending time with people as a sign of appreciation, not giving them gifts. He would probably think, "Well, nice, but why don't we just go out and you could buy me a few beers at the pub instead of just giving me something and walking away?" It's just not his language. If you want to be effective communicator, don't show people appreciation in your language, **do it in their language**, provided you've known them long enough. My dear wife, for example, likes being surprised very much. When I buy her a present for a special occasion, she appreciates it, but no matter how much love I give her, she feels a little bit neglected when I don't positively surprise her once in a while (and that doesn't have to mean buying stuff, she just loves the surprise factor and unpredictability showed in many different ways). Don't treat people the way you like to be treated, treat them the way THEY want to be treated. That's a **big** rapport take-away to remember!

Leading

In addition to matching, the concept of rapport includes **leading**.

As soon as you establish a good strong connection, you can start leading. If you have deep rapport with a person, you've succeeded already. Now you can take the next step. Thanks to that you will be able to exert influence on people, changing their emotional states and approach to various issues. For example, if someone is stressed out and you want them to be relaxed—first you adjust to that stressed out state, and then you begin to change your attitude to a more relaxed one. Slowly you begin to speak more slowly, breathe deeply and do less intense gestures.

If you do it skillfully and not obviously, the other person will start to follow, and you are going to lead them towards a better, more pleasant emotional state. This is a really great tool that gives huge opportunities in terms of effective communication.

Some will say that they "prefer to be themselves" and that they believe such actions are artificial. Sticking rigidly to the same behavior can sometimes bring good results, but it's on the contrary much more often. Now you have obtained knowledge which allows you to achieve excellent results in many different situations. Remember that every single interaction with the other person has a purpose.

The objectives can be different: getting close to the other person, gaining trust, comforting the person, exchanging viewpoints and many others. Whatever the goal, rapport helps you achieve it by establishing better contact with other people. Creation of harmony and effective agreement is a beautiful thing, and what's more, brings great benefits for both sides of communication.

Chapter 15: How to Use Metaphors to Communicate Better

Our daily conversations are stuffed with this remarkable linguistic structure—on average, during one minute of spoken language, we usually use as many as six metaphors. Once you learn to notice metaphors among other people's words, magical things start to happen.

The ability of referring to metaphors in daily conversation gives you many great new possibilities: everything from changing other people's beliefs, or solving their problems, to inducing laughter or motivation. In this chapter I will show you how to navigate among metaphors during your usual conversations, coaching sessions or even business negotiations.

Metaphors vs. Logical Mind

Imagine that your friend says: "My business is not taking off!" As long as this person is not actually a pilot or airline owner, they're referring to a specific event or situation in their life. Maybe you could simply ignore the metaphor and just ask, "What do you mean?" However, getting very clear information about how this problem is represented in their mind and then relating to this specific metaphor gives a much better effect. Why? Because then their logical mind doesn't get into action, ruining all your efforts.

The fight with their logical mind in such a situation would be rather a futile attempt. Your friend, explaining to you what exactly they meant by saying their business isn't taking off, would find a lot of reasonable arguments supporting this metaphor and possibly start feeling even worse. "...Oh, I'm so hopeless! Can't even take care of my own business!" Even if you were brilliant with rhetoric and turned down all of these self-depreciating arguments one by one, they would probably find new ones. More or less accurate, but quite true for their logical mind.

By referring to a metaphor itself, **you bypass your interlocutor's conscious mind and refer to their subconscious.** The world of metaphors is created subconsciously and usually has no direct connection with the real issue it presents.

Thanks to this, there is almost no risk that the so-called "inner critic" (internal voice) will start messing around in this person's head, making them feel even worse. It is impossible to discuss with a metaphor!

Move Inside the Metaphor

What does "moving across the metaphor" mean? This is the process of taking a particular metaphor literally and referring to it as if it was not a metaphor, but a normal, logical expression.

Let's discuss it on the example of our friend's business "not taking off." Knowing how beneficial referring to a metaphor usually is, instead of asking for specific reasons for not taking off, you could ask, "Are you sure that you accelerated your plane to the maximum speed before trying to take off?", or, "How long is the airstrip?" You can also ask, "In that case, what can you do to make the engines run at top speed and finally take off?", or, "Have you read the right manual on how to fly this particular plane?"

There are many options. Going further, you could also say, "Maybe you need to try taking off with a better, newer model plane?" Or with humor, "Are you sure that you're sitting inside of a plane? Maybe it's just a strange car?" Each of these metaphors proposes different solutions or invites the other person to discover a particular issue more deeply. "Next time you better refuel your plane before trying to take off, or you will just drive all around the runway again and make ground control laugh!"

The most unusual thing about metaphors is that the **subconscious mind will always find the relevant and necessary meaning of a particular analogy.** It often happens that two different people find answers for two different problems (which don't have anything in common) in a single metaphor. High flexibility of this fanciful linguistic structure makes it useful in a plethora of situations. Maybe that's why it's so widely used in many religious books and folklore stories. It's very helpful for our mind and our ancestors knew about it.

Some time ago a friend and coworker told me: "I feel like I have had my hands tied with a thick rope for a very long time..." I asked him: "Do you want to run all over the place and beg people to cut these ropes and free your hands, or maybe you will finally pull yourself together, find a sharp hook and tear them up to shreds?" He just nodded his head significantly and said, "I definitely prefer to find the inner strength and opportunity to tear these cords up." This brief exchange of thoughts made me realize very quickly who I'm dealing with and how to talk to him to get him motivated to overcome his problems.

Remember that before you start referring to a metaphor, it is worth to have a good rapport with your conversation partner.

The strategy of referring to metaphors used in everyday conversation is very simple and consists of two stages:

1. Specification of a metaphor.

2. Searching for solutions.

In both stages you move only on the surface of the metaphor, not going into the details of what the particular analogy means for the person you are talking with.

To explain it better, let me tell you about a case described by Sue Knight in her book, *NLP at Work*. She worked with this company where the CEOs would often use these expressions in conversations between themselves:

- "I was taking heavy fire..."

- "To attack the competition..."

- "Aim at the right spot..."

This way of perceiving their business wasn't too a beneficial cognitive scheme in this instance. Instead of focusing on how to improve their company, these CEOs were focusing on their "enemies" and the "war" they believed they led. They were wasting their energy on the constant preparation for the "fight" instead of putting their focus on finding new, creative ways to make their business stand out.

Taking the two stages of working with metaphors into account, I would ask them questions like: "Who is fighting with whom here?", "What are you fighting for?", "How will you know that you won the war?" and so on.

Knowing the answers, I would refer to searching for solutions through some ideas that are still connected with the metaphors of war or battle. I could also use more general solutions: "Wouldn't it be better if you buried the hatchet, or perhaps maybe even joined your forces at some point?", "You will never build a great empire focusing on fighting all the time. Perhaps it would be better to put the entire focus in development inside of the team?"

If you refer to a given problem like that, it's almost guaranteed that you will be understood by the person who sees the world in a certain way. You do not have to have a huge knowledge or specific skills to give a good metaphoric solution, as metaphors are usually simple.

Below you will find is a list of some other metaphors which are often used by people in conversations. Take a look at the list to be able to notice them easier in conversations. In addition, taking each of them into consideration, you can practice what you have learned in this chapter:

- I'm carrying a huge weight on my shoulders.

- I have a feeling that there is a big, thick wall in front of me.

- Someone cut my wings.

- I am speechless.

- I am still standing in the same place and cannot move forward.

- We do not transmit on the same wavelengths.

- He's like a ticking time bomb.

Where Can You Use This Knowledge?

- In any conversation, with any person in order to play with the language and improve your linguistic skills. Catch metaphors, change them, seek solutions and make others laugh.

- When you want to help someone - people very often describe their problems with the help of metaphors. Expand on metaphors they use and try to find better solutions for them on the level of these analogies.

- To influence and inspire others - when someone verbalizes some of their obstacles/blocks in the form of a metaphor (e.g. "it's out of my league"), refer to it without getting into logical arguments and open that person to new possibilities.

- When you want to teach someone or open their eyes to something important - a good metaphor can be the key to understand even the most difficult issues. It's sometimes enough if you start a sentence with: "It's just as if..." to make someone's mind "click."

These are just few ideas on how to apply operations on the level of metaphors. Across the vast ocean of possibilities, you will surely find out what is the most useful for you.

The world of metaphors is truly fascinating and I encourage you to start discovering it—**mastery of this particular linguistic structure in conversations takes communication to a totally new level.**

Chapter 16: Metaprograms

Do you want to know the key to every human's mind? Metaprograms refer to the different ways of filtering incoming information by different people. Knowledge about specific mental filters they use gives you the opportunity to communicate much more effectively with others and also enables you to really strengthen the influence you have on them.

As you already know from first chapters of this book, everyone makes decisions, finds solutions, processes what you say or motivates themselves differently. The ability to see these differences and to recognize different metaprograms allows you to adjust your message so that you can always reach the intended goal of your interaction.

The human mind processes a HUGE amount of information every single moment of our lives. To be able to function normally in this world, it must filter all the information and signals it receives by ignoring some of them and letting others in. **Metaprograms are these filters of perception, which decide how we develop specific, individual thinking patterns in our brains.** They are a little bit like club bouncers, defining which information will be let in and which won't be allowed to enter.

Neuro-Linguistic Programming (NLP) assumes that every person has their own unique set of metaprograms. They filter the world of every person differently, creating unique maps of reality. Metaprograms define how each person will behave in a particular situation.

Metaprograms can be easily identified by the observation of behavior and language a particular person uses. The ability to see the patterns between different metaprograms gives really amazing opportunities in communication with others—you can easily tell which decision to make, how to motivate people and how to look at their specific problems. **Such knowledge allows you to customize your message for the receiver, having much more of an impact on their behavior.**

In his book Introducing NLP, Joseph O'Connor writes: "A good speaker forms his message the way it fits the other person's world. He uses language compatible with their metaprograms, changing the shape of information in advance and making sure that they will be able to understand it easily."

Let me show you the most important metaprograms now. I'll describe them thoroughly so you have a clear picture of what each of them is about. In addition, I will show you the way to recognize each metaprogram in the other person and the way to use this knowledge in a smart way.

Motivation From-To

This metaprogram refers to **a strategy of motivating oneself**. People with a "TO" metaprogram are focused on their goals, while those with a pattern of "FROM" are focused on the problems to avoid. The former ones motivate themselves more easily when they have an image of something positive in their minds, something they can achieve, a success they can reach. **They are attracted TO this image.** On the other hand, people with "FROM" metaprograms motivate themselves by being constantly aware of what bad can happen if they do not execute on a particular task. **They motivate themselves using fear, are pushed away FROM the negative images.**

How do you recognize these metaprograms? For example, when a person works a day job, you can ask why they chose that work over another field. Depending on which pattern is more dominant in them, they will answer that either this work allows them to achieve their goals and realize their dreams, or that this job gives them a roof over their head and allows them to pay their bills. Of course that might not apply in every possible case of people working day jobs, as some of these dead-end jobs don't leave space for any self-development and everyone knows it, but you get the point. If the person you are talking to does not work yet, you can ask about their reason for choosing a particular university, school, or faculty over another, why they do what they do, etc. Besides, this metaprogram very often appears in usual, everyday conversations.

Once you recognize the pattern usually used by this person, you gain the possibility to influence and motivate them much more effectively. **When persuading that person to do something, always use their metaprogram.** Trying to motivate someone with strong desire for accomplishments and successes by some kind of punishment will be ineffective in most cases or could even bring opposite effect. And vice versa, if you try to use some kind of reward to motivate people who always think about how to avoid defeats, it may end up in a failure. Of course, this rule is not an absolute when applied, at least not always and everywhere, but remembering about the matching of metaprograms you will always be sure that your message will have the planned effect or at least end up close to it.

Similarities-Differences

People who are similarly oriented will notice things similar to each other in many different contexts, whereas those focused on differences filter their reality mainly by noticing new, different and various things. The first group of people usually do not like changes, stay away from new technologies and revolutionary solutions. The second group of people looks for changes, likes challenges, and likes to grow.

What kind of relations do you notice between these three triangles? A similarities-oriented person would probably say that these three triangles are the same size and same color, while the person differences-oriented one can respond to the same question that two triangles are the same, and another one is different—upside down. You can try it on someone by, for instance, showing them three coins, two showing tails, and one heads.

Looking from a point of language, people with the metaprogram of similarity often use the phrases: "the same," "similar," "traditionally" or "commonly." People with metaprograms of differences use phrases such as: "different," "various," "innovative" or "as opposed to."

Let's suppose that you are a car seller. A person comes to you who owns the same model that you are currently selling, just from three years prior, and now is looking for a new model. If this man is focused on the similarities, it will be much easier to convince him into buying the new model by telling him it retains all the advantages of its predecessors, that it is still the same tradition, that the very soul of this car remains unchanged. On the other hand, if that person is focused on the differences it is worth it to say: "This model is completely new, has an innovative line, many revolutionary features, much better acceleration, it's almost an entirely different car that just looks a little bit alike."

The two metaprograms above refer mainly to motivation. Fluency in noticing them quickly will help you motivate and persuade people you are communicating with much more effectively and quickly by adjusting your message to your receiver. Start to watch and listen to people during each conversation more carefully—you should be able to notice these patterns quite quickly. Often it's possible to differentiate metaprograms of the other people even during the most usual conversation about the weather.

Knowing how the mind of another human filters information allows your messages to be much more precise, which is the key to effective motivation and influencing.

Options/Procedures

People focused on options like to have a possibility of choice. They avoid common schemes and feel much better when they have big impact on the process of achieving their goals.

People focused on the procedures prefer to work according to the finished procedure scheme or template, without feeling the urge to make their own choices. They feel best when their tasks are determined in advance and they accomplish what has to be done step by step following, for example, some kind of written outline.

People focused on options are more often very creative. It is not the best idea to employ them on positions where success depends strictly on the adherence to superiors' commands. Figuratively, it is not worth it to employ people focused on procedures where more creative ways of acting and individual decision making are needed.

For instance, when you want to convince a person focused on "options" to do something, tell them about a wide range of opportunities they will have in this position. Show them where they will be able to make decisions for themselves, and how big their impact on the course of the whole situation will be. Show that they will be able to use their own ideas. When interviewing a person focused on procedures, let them know they will receive all the detailed instructions necessary to operate. Convince them that everything will be clear and well-presented, and the only thing that they will have to do is execute the ready-to-use instructions.

General/Detailed

People with "general" metaprogram prefer to look at the whole problem or issue in general from a bigger perspective. They feel good when they can fully embrace the concept. **People oriented on the details, however, prefer to look at the specific elements of the whole.** They focus the greatest attention on details, on the specific elements of problems and concepts.

The former are usually great at planning. Their ability to grasp all issues allows them to prepare a plan and a strategy for better action. People with a "detailed" metaprogram feel best in tasks which are a sequence of individual steps are required. They look at each single task individually, focusing only on one step at a time.

Again, this metaprogram can easily be learned by observing peoples' expressions. Listen carefully any time they are presenting an issue, problem or idea. Note if they are talking about the details and specific elements of this issue or are rather focused on general transmission of the concept.

How can you use this knowledge? Let's suppose that you are a bicycles retailer. If your customer is focused on the general perspective, you could encourage them by speaking about the general merits of this bike (it will allow them to take long and enjoyable trips, they will feel great riding this bike, that it's comfortable and robust, etc.). To a person with "detailed" metaprogram you could say that this bike has great brakes, handlebars, and a frame made from the best materials, essentially only the concrete stuff.

The Authority of the External/Internal

People oriented to external authority need the support of others to make a decision. They usually lean on the authority in a particular field. When they have to make a decision, they ask other people for their opinion, and based on their feedback, they make their final decision. **Those oriented to the internal authority rely**

only and exclusively on their own beliefs on the subject. They reject the opinion of others, taking mainly their own priorities and judgments into consideration. Generally, they are guided by their own guts.

People with a metaprogram of "external authority" need someone who is going to support them and show them the right way. Those on the opposite side can rarely accept someone else's leadership.

How can you specify this metaprogram in another person? The most helpful question might be, "How do you know that you've done your job well?" People with the internal authority will say that they rated it themselves, while those with an external authority will indicate the confirmation from other people.

In an attempt to convince someone into something, you can tell them about how they will have your support or the support of other people along the way, and they will always be able to ask for an advice and help at any moment. You can also convince internal-authority people by telling them about how much independence and real impact they will have on the decision-making process by selecting the most suitable options for them, et cetera.

Me/Others

The last metaprogram which I'm going to describe refers to the particular view of benefits. **People with the "me" metaprogram usually focus on their benefits as opposed to people with the "others" metaprogram, which mainly pay attention to what other people's benefits will be.**

This metaprogram is very easy to recognize. Asking people what benefits are the most important to them, you'll notice that some people talk mainly about themselves, or about other people, for example, about their loved ones. Someone focused on "me" will say, "I want to be happy about it," "I'm doing it for myself," or, "I need this." Someone with "others" metaprogram will say, "I want other people to like it," "I care about the opinion of my friends," "My wife has to accept it," or maybe, "I won't buy this product— I like it but I'm concerned about the environment."

Once you recognize which direction this person takes, use it to talk about the benefits for that person, or about the benefits for people from their surroundings.

Recognition of metaprograms is very easy—**you just need to ask the right questions and carefully listen to the answers.** In most cases, these questions are not even necessary, because usual conversations quickly reveal particular patterns.

Remember that metaprograms are, after all, mainly about generalizations. If you recognize particular metaprograms in someone, it obviously **doesn't mean they will always behave like this.** Metaprograms may change over time, and also according to different contexts. **Therefore, be observant and flexible; do not attach yourself to one metaprogram** when you discover that, for example, a person close to you is detail-oriented. There might also be some individuals who are not completely specified by a single side of a particular metaprogram. They may be more in the middle, oscillating between one and another.

Hence, remember to **carefully listen to the other person's words all the time**, not only until the moment you specify their metaprograms for the first time. **Do not put people into boxes, but rather assume that the person is using the particular metaprogram at that moment, and that is why and when you can use it.**

Use your head when trying to put your influence on others, bearing in mind the fact that the key to effective communication is matching your message to the way in which other people communicate. Therefore, respect their metaprograms and benefit from this knowledge. Wisely used, this may prove to be an extremely powerful tool. Practice checking what works best in which context. Remember that when you learn how to utilize this knowledge in practice, you will naturally become very familiar with it at some point and you will become even better communicator.

Chapter 17: Meta Model

Meta Model is a pillar of the linguistic part of NLP. Mastery of this concept will help you to improve your communication with others but also enable you to cope with your own beliefs.

Let me begin by telling you more about the concept of Meta Model and the assumptions built on its foundations so you become familiar with the most important language structures and questions, which can be used to undermine limiting beliefs—both yours and the people's with whom you communicate.

Meta Model is the work of Richard Bandler and John Grinder. For a few years they observed and analyzed the actions of the best psychotherapists they knew. On the basis **of Fritz Persl's, Virginia Satir's and Milton Erickson's work** they created the linguistic therapeutic model, which allows for effective problem solving during the therapy. You can find a very exact description of the Meta Model in Richard Bandler's book The Structure of Magic, which was also his PhD thesis work. It's a great read.

To understand what the Meta Model is, it is worth the time to familiarize yourself with the concepts of deep structure and surface structure, which describe the formation of mental representations in an easier way.

Using our senses, we receive "raw material" from the world around us—what we see, hear, feel, taste and smell. **All of this sensual information is a deep structure.** It's everything that we receive from the outside world, without mental interpretation. In order to function in the world around us, we need to simplify the raw material, because otherwise we wouldn't able to embrace the whole.

We use language to represent our experience, as well as to communicate it. Using language, we create maps of reality and this is the advantage we have over other animals. **Our map of reality, which is a simplified version of raw experience, is the surface structure.** We respond to it on a daily basis. It's our beliefs and thoughts about the surrounding reality.

People who are successful and enjoy life in general are able to draw from the world in a direct manner. They do not dilute their experience by passing them through the filters of what they "should" experience or what they expect to experience.

A lot of people go to the cinema to see a movie with a set of beliefs about it. They were formed on the basis of the trailer, written reviews or the opinions of their friends. These filters make them receive the film differently than they would have received it if they saw it without creating the initial assumptions.

On many different levels of our lives, we look at the world through the prism of an entire set of generalizations, distortions and deletions.

Meta Model is a set of linguistic structures that are mainly questions, and it's thanks to them we are able to obtain information that has been "hidden." We hide this information because then it is easier for us to communicate with others—we can provide each other generalized information. Unfortunately, it often raises problems because we react to false beliefs that were formed as a result of the creation of a general image of reality.

While you create a map of reality from the raw experience, there are three main processes: **removal (or deletion), generalizations and distortions.** Each of these processes cut out some information from our communication, and that's why it is more difficult for us to communicate and understand each other.

In therapy or coaching, a Meta Model is used to help people experience the deep structure again. That is, the full description of a given situation. Responding to generalized thought patterns can often be the main or even only source of destructive feelings.

Deletions:

Deletion is the skipping of information that is relevant in a given situation.

- **Simple Deletion** – Speaking highly generally.

"I'm disappointed."

What exactly disappointed you? What happened? What were you expecting?

- **Comparison** – Removal of information essential in comparing ourselves with others.

"They are better than me!"

Who specifically? What are they better at? How are they better?

- **The Lack of Benchmark** – There's no noun in the expression. People involved in the situation have not been named.

"I was warned..."

Who was threatening you? Who warned you about it?

- **Indefinite Benchmark** – Those involved were listed in a general way.

"They cheated me!"

Who is cheating on you? How did they cheat on you?

- **Unspecified Verb** – The problem mentioned is not specified.

"She is hurting me by doing this."

What exactly did she do? How did she hurt you?

Distortions:

Changing of a given situation or phenomenon's meaning.

- **Nominalization** – Changing a verb to a noun, reducing the whole process to a single thing or event.

"I'm down."

How did you down yourself? This question also helps to regain responsibility for the process.

- **Cause-Effect (A Causes B)** – Explanation of one situation with another, which does not have a direct cause-effect with it.

"He doesn't listen to me, so he doesn't care about me."

Does he never listen to you? How is one related to the other? Do you always listen to him?

- **Mind Reading** – Supporting your expressions with your conjectures and projections about the thoughts of other people.

"She thinks that I am hopeless."

How exactly do you know that? What does she tell you about it?

- **Complex Equivalent (A = B)** – Where event A supposedly causes event B, but it's

only true for that person due to their beliefs and attitude.

"Christmas without snow is hopeless."

How does one cause the other?

- Anonymous Authority – Supporting of the statement with an authority which has never been specified.

"We should not talk about this."

According to whom? Who said so?

Generalizations:

Generalizations of phenomena and situations on the basis of a single or few experiences.

- Numerals – "Always," "all," "everyone," "no one," "none."

"All entrepreneurs struggle with financial liquidity."

Absolutely everyone? Do you know all of the entrepreneurs in our country and in the world?

- Modal Operators – "I must," "I should," "I can't."

"I can't let it happen."

What stands in the way? What or who is holding you back? What exactly will happen if you do it?

- Presumptions – Hidden assumptions.

"Before you judge me, first think about what kind of man you are yourself."

Where did the assumption that I will be judging you come from?

For me, the Meta Model has always been one of the most important parts of the entire NLP and the art of effective communication. I learned it to such an extent that it became a section of my unconscious mind, and so I use it naturally, spontaneously when I need it as a part of my competence. At a certain stage, good questions come intuitively. It is a very useful tool during coaching sessions.

Meta Model is one of the main topics within the framework of the majority of NLP trainings. For me, it's one of the most crucial ones.

It is important to use Meta Model subtly and with moderation. The continuous asking of (even right) questions may be uncomfortable for your conversation partners, because not everyone is willing to expose or admit imperfections of their thinking. Meta Model should serve you to improve communication. Therefore, remember not to overuse it. You don't want to interrogate people. Always take care of the <u>rapport</u> with your interlocutor and feel if they're ready for a conversation, which to some extent can be therapeutic.

You can practice the Meta Model with someone who also wants to learn it. Make a list of limiting beliefs and ask each other questions from this chapter. This way, you will quickly get familiar with it and you will be able to intuitively choose appropriate questions.

Chapter 18: Eye Accessing Cues

Do you know that eye movements can show whether someone thinks by images, sounds or feelings? "Sensory predicates and eye accessing cues" is a model of how man gets access to a specific type of information which is stored somewhere in the subconscious.

This assumption, developed by the creators of NLP, is based on the knowledge that the information related to specific senses is stored in different areas of our brain. Watching the eyes of the other person, you may be able to determine quite accurately what is happening in their heads!

Perhaps you have already noticed that people sometimes look in a few different directions while conversing with you. You were probably convinced that these looks are either random or something attracted their attention. For some instances this could indeed be so. However, in most cases, this person probably tried to **access some information,** reaching into their memory, imagining the picture or speaking to themselves in their minds.

Sometimes, when people tell you about their recent summer vacations, they look up and to their left. Such eye movements are usually subconscious reflex action which helps them remind themselves, for example, how the view from the top of Eiffel tower looked.

Another time, someone looks down and to their left side, wanting to recall what someone told to them. They are obtaining access to information stored as an internal dialogue, which is simply an audio projection of a memory.

This knowledge allows you to discover what is currently happening in the mind of the other person. Of course, you are not able to find out what exactly this person is thinking about and it's not really a mind-reading technique per se, but knowing whether it is a picture, sound or a feeling gives you some great opportunities.

How does it work?

The vast majority of information we receive from the outside world is stored by our subconscious. Any time we want to access this database we have to "move" the "files" from there to our consciousness. Sensory predicates and eye accessing cues tell us about the way in which most people reach for this information. This, of course, is a generalization, which is not true for all people in the world—but surprisingly often this model really goes along with what we experience.

The process of obtaining access to information is made either through a brief look in a particular direction, or by looking there for a longer moment, reflecting on the answer. It is worth remembering that a look in a certain direction doesn't have to be made for the person to access specific memory—it is only a subconscious facilitation for a brain.

On the diagram below you can see the directions people look to gain access to a particular type of information.

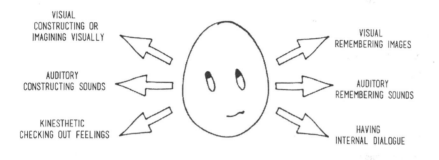

(This is what you see when you look at the other person)

As mentioned earlier, the above diagram is a generalization, which means that it doesn't always have to be like that. However, even if a person is looking in another direction than the diagram states, usually the sensory predicates and eye accessing cues will be permanent and fixed for them. So, for example, looking to their left to remember sounds. The next time they want to access the same type of information, they will quite likely look in the same direction as it's a fixed habit type of process.

Directions may also vary in left-handed people—what should be on left will usually be located on the right side. Remember that since the human brain is the most complicated mechanism known to man, you cannot take anything for granted during interpersonal relations. Always carefully watch the person with whom you are speaking.

I would not recommend using this model as a lie detection tool. I met some NLP-freaks who believed that if they ask, "What were you doing last week at this exact time?" and the person pauses to think of the answer while looking to their right side and up, then they're lying as they're creating an image instead of remembering it. This interpretation, however, may be far from the truth. Why?

Sometimes some of our memories are blurred or faded and we help ourselves by creating images. Sometimes when you ask someone about what their best friend's voice sounds like, they will first look up creating a picture of the friend, and then down forming the sound of their voice. You need to take a lot of different options into account, so you can never be 100% sure about your interpretation, even after extensive CIA interrogation training. Moreover, some people are just extraordinarily talented at lying.

Let's do a little experiment.

Anticipating that you will probably want to try it in practice, I have prepared for you a few questions that will allow you to test this model on another person. To each symptom, you will find three questions that correspond to a particular type of information. When you manage to convince someone to do this experiment, in any case, do not tell this person anything about eye movements or about anything that is really the subject of this "research". Simply say that you want to ask them a few questions.

Reminded Images:

- What color are the walls in your room?

- What do you see from the window in your office?

- What color was your t-shirt yesterday?

Created Images:

- How would your room look with pink polka dots on the wall?

- What would an elephant cross-bred with a tiger look like?

- Imagine a green square in a red triangle.

Reminded Sounds:

- What sound does the door to your room make when it slams?

- What is the ringtone you have set on your phone?

- What is the sound of your closest friend's voice?

Created Sounds:

- How would a radio sound underwater?

- What sound would a drunk bird make?

- How would a scream made by five thousand people at one time sound?

Kinesthetic (Feelings):

- How does holding a snowball in your hand feel?

- How does it feel to dip your hand in a bathtub full of hot water?

- What do you feel when you touch sandpaper?

Internal Dialogue:

- What do you say to yourself when something does not go the way you want it?

- What tone of voice do you have when you're talking to yourself?

- Tell yourself something nice in your thoughts.

Ask these questions to someone else rather than yourself, because staring in a specific direction when accessing information is a process of the subconscious. If you ask yourself these questions thinking simultaneously about where you are looking, you will disturb this natural process. It is best to ask these questions to a person who is not familiar with NLP, communication techniques, is not a police officer, special agent, psychotherapist, etc. During this exercise, do not tell this person what it is about until you finish asking all the questions.

It is important that you get familiar with the ability to see even the smallest glances, as sometimes they only last for a part of a second. You have to be very attentively focused on observing what's happening on the other person's face.

If the person who you are asking questions to gives you the answers quickly, without looking in various directions, it is worth it to ask them more detailed questions which will force them to think. For example, "What color were the walls painted before the last renovation?", "What color are the walls in the basement?", or, "What if this hybrid of an elephant and tiger somehow also gets crossed with a hamster? What would it look like?" Play with these questions a little bit and have fun. More detailed or abstract questions will force your interlocutor to think deeply and will eventually cause eye movements.

When I decided to test this model with this set of questions on a few people, it worked on 5 out of 8 cases. I was very positively surprised by the result. Now, watching people as I ask them questions (no longer in the context of the experiment, but simply during usual conversations) I often notice how unconsciously their eyes "escape" when they are looking for answers and it mostly sticks to what you see above.

This little trick can also be useful:

- When identifying whether a person thinks with images, sounds or feelings, which allows you for **better communication and building a good rapport**. For instance, by using language of the senses, "See, it's as clear as the summer sky!"

- When **referring to what someone said by using gestures,** e.g., "When you were relaxing on that beatiful beach, did you..." and point with your hand in the same direction or spot that person looked at while recalling their holiday.

- **As a fun fact,** showing others interesting information about how our mind works.

Discover it yourself by checking how frequently it works in reality. Consider where else you can find it useful and use it as much as possible!

You can also take a look at this clip on YouTube, it's a really good example of this subconscious reaction:

http://tinyurl.com/eyecues

Chapter 19: How to Predict Future Behaviors

In this short but useful chapter I'm going to show you one of my favorite tricks that few people know about: how to predict how anyone will act in the future. It's invaluable in many different situations, such as work interviews, dating, business meetings, etc. Have you ever been asked annoying and pointless questions during job interviews, such as, "So tell me about your approach to work," or, "Where do you see yourself in five years?" Well, by asking these questions, people usually want to learn something about your future behaviors and your mindset, but since no one would respond, "I don't give a crap about work and you know that; all I need is your money and my peace after five," or, "In five years I see myself chilling out in Tahiti with drink in my hand," these questions usually don't make any real sense and aren't asked by HR professionals who know what they're doing nor by effective communicators.

Don't just ask people things like, "So, tell me how you deal with conflicts?" because what you are going to get is a bland and pointless answer, crafted so that you hear what you want to hear. Unfortunately, their real behavior will be revealed only during the real conflict. Do you want to know what is most likely to show you future behaviors? **Past behavior—the best future predictor!** If you are about to ask someone a question that is intended to discover how they are going to act in a variety of different situations, what you are going to do is to use this simple process: first of all, you need to ask them about a specific situation that happened in the past. Then, you want to ask them how they reacted initially to this situation. Lastly, you need to ask them how they resolved this situation.

So, for example, you might ask: "Tell me about a time in the past when you found yourself in the middle of a conflict about something very important to you. How did you react to that conflict, how did you go about resolving it and how did you work through that conflict?" When you ask questions formed like that, you force people to stop for a moment and really think about the specific conflict they were in, how they reacted, what steps they took and how they eventually resolved it. That's when you're really going to find out what they are going to do when a similar challenge arises with you or in your company/department/relationship/etc. That is going to be a great new skill to accompany you throughout your life. For example, if your date would tell you that she had a conflict in a previous marriage, found out that her husband was gambling and that the first thing she did was apply for a divorce without even listening to what he had to say, you would know that this person has a short fuse and is not really into long-term problem-solving, and if she finds out something she doesn't like, she will probably dump you in a second. With an answer like, "Well, I went online, found a good family psychotherapist and we went to our first meeting the very next day," you would know she's proactive and into conflict-solving. You can use this in all varieties of different professional and personal situations. So don't ask, "What would you do?" or, "How do you come about..." Instead, ask about certain situations from the past, using this format: "What happened, how did you react, how did you resolve it or how did that turn out?" With this simple but powerful upgrade in your communication, you are going to feel like a sorcerer or an oracle. You will be surprised to see how often people do exactly the same things they did in the past.

Chapter 20: How to Finally Start Remembering Names?

The ability to quickly and permanently remember peoples' names is an **extremely** underrated skill and a must-have feature of anyone who wants to communicate effectively and smoothly! Remembering names will allow you to make an awesome first impression and save you lots of trouble that you might find after forgetting someone's name after five minutes of conversation.

Some time ago, remembering names was a great challenge for me. Usually when two or three people told me their names, I forgot them after about a few minutes. I really wanted to remember them, but they would just vanish rapidly. It very often held me back from making a good first impression and from succeeding at job interviews, during the first days at a new school, university, in a new company, during business meetings or even during nights out with friends when I wanted to meet new people. From what I noticed, this is quite a popular problem. My dear friend almost lost the chance to have a date with the love of his life because he forgot her name and after one hour of talking, called her Jennifer instead of Jessica. It ended up in a painful but funny (for us, not him) face slap since she is rather a fiery and impulsive kind of girl. Luckily, I eventually managed to convince her that he's a very good man, just a little bit forgetful. I'm going to show you a few tricks thanks to which you will be able to impress everyone with your great memory for names and improve your social skills.

Remembering a name and then using it early in the first conversations is one of the best ways to make a **great first impression.** By using the name of the person who you just met, you will make them feel important to you. By doing so, you can easily open the door to creating a special relationship with that person.

"For most people their own name is the sweetest and most important sound in any language." - **Dale Carnegie**

Here's how to go about it:

1. Commit Yourself

Decide today that you will remember names every time you meet someone new. Usually, when we talk to someone for the first time, we do not pay attention to their name. It usually disappears from our heads literally in a matter of seconds. That's why **the commitment** to start remembering the names of people you meet is so important.

If you think, "I have such a bad memory for names," then you are wrong and looking for excuses. There is no such thing as a bad memory for names. If you do not remember them, it means that you do nothing to remember them. Decide that from now on you will start doing something in this direction. Recall that undertaking whenever you expect to meet someone new.

2. Focus

When you are greeting someone for the first time, always be focused on this activity. You need to be present in the moment. Dispersion and lack of focused attention will simply hold you back from remembering names. Carefully listen to what people say, how they introduce themselves. Moreover, take notice of how each person looks. See what characteristics their faces have. You will need these details to create associations, which I will describe in the fourth point.

3. Repeat

Repetition of the name is a quick way to save it in your memory. You can repeat names in many different ways. For example, immediately using the given name. Let's suppose that someone introduces himself to you as Adam. And you say: "Hi Adam, nice to meet you." After a while of conversation you might ask, "Listen Adam, you've got really cool accent, are you from...?" Another way to repeat the name is pronouncing it in your thoughts. In this case, after Adam introduces himself, you say in your head, "Adam, Adam, Adam, Adam, Adam, Adam..." The third possibility is to write this name on a piece of paper as soon as you have the opportunity to do so. Of course it depends on the circumstances in which you meet, but you can always save that name in your cellphone or somewhere else. The mere act of writing it will help your memory by a great degree.

4. Create Associations

Whenever you hear new name, create images which include the associations of the name with an object or event. In addition, make this image vivid, funny, or even absurd and overdrawn, colorful and in motion—it will make you remember this picture and the name connected with it much better.

A few examples:

- You just met **Caroline**. Imagine her wearing a big, colorful necklace of coral beads. These corals are heavy, have a strange shape and bright colors. She bought this necklace in South Carolina.

-You just met **Adam**. Imagine him dressed as a dignified lady. She wears a long and beautiful dress and has a fan in her hand, which she uses for cooling herself. Now that it's not Adam, you should address him madam!

- **Kenny**. You just checked your pockets and you have no cash! You ask Kenny to lend you a penny, so you can grab a nice cold beer together.

- **Ann**. Imagine Ann dressed as a police officer and holding a gun. She has an oversized police hat on her head and a scared robber handcuffed to her wrist. Ann and her big gun.

As you can see, it's pretty simple. Anyone can create such funny or silly associations in a few seconds. When you do this, **keep the created image in your head for a few seconds.** Now if you have to remind yourself a particular name, the association will come immediately to your mind.

Note that you can create specific associations with many names. Then, for example, when you meet another Caroline, you will already know which image to use, without a need to create a new one each time. I believe that this is a great idea, but since I find it quite amusing to come up with new ideas every single time, I did not decide on doing this too often.

5. Ask Again

If for some reason you could not use these techniques, or you've somehow already forgotten the name someone you've just met—**don't be afraid to ask them to repeat their name.** This person certainly will be happy to tell you their name again.

It's much better solution than allowing for a situation in which you will have to use that name for a few hours, and it's gone.

You can use all of these ideas at the same time, however in most cases you only need one technique (numbers 3 or 4). Therefore, it is best to first test each of them individually. **See which one works best for you and stay with it.** Using both repeating and associations is a sure way to always remember new names.

When I meet new people and we're still chatting, my strategy is to use their name often in conversation and additionally repeat it in my memory. As soon as I finish talking with them and I have a free moment, I create some funny association in my mind.

When the problem of remembering names is gone, you need to remember one more thing. **Use these names!** You have to show people that you remember their names. That's why when you ask someone about something, you should use their name as part of the question. If you stopped talking with them and you want to ask them about something again, start a sentence by saying their name. As this person hears their name and realizes that you already remember it despite the fact you have just met, it will be a very enjoyable experience for them. You will make a great impression on them and your conversation will be taken to a completely different level.

Chapter 21: 16 Ways to Have a Great Public Presentation

The ability to act in front of a bigger group of people is one of the most desired skills among people interested in self-development. It's because we perform all the time—not only during presentations, business meetings or trainings, but also in normal everyday situations, like when we meet up with our friends.

There are a lot of ways to make your presentation unique and remembered by all listeners.

During my HR and coaching careers I had the opportunity to commit many errors, thanks to which I learned more than from any books I read. This allowed me to consistently develop my skills and led to the point at which I can share with you with the knowledge gained from my personal experience so you can always achieve goals you have set for yourself while giving public performances and speeches.

Depending on the context in which you will use and benefit from this unique skill, your goals may be different. Among a group of friends, your intention may be to make all of them roll on the floor laughing. During business presentations it can be showing your listeners a vivid vision of your idea, which they can see clearly and understand entirely. During school or college speeches it could be evoking a strong state of curiosity, so that the students and professors listen to every word you say.

In short, you will be able to show yourself from the best side, presenting what you have in an interesting way and having a great time while doing it, along with your audience.

Here are 16 ways to carry out a great presentation:

1. **Prepare the material, but do not learn it by heart.** It is best to take a general outline of what you want to say and select the most important bullet points of your presentation. Use colors and underlines or drawings when you create this sketch, so you can easily recall bullet points and things you need to speak about. If you still forget them during your rehearsal, let the sheet lie somewhere nearby so you can look at it and immediately know what to say. There are two reasons to avoid holding pieces of

paper in your hands during a presentation: firstly, you are blocking your hands and have limited opportunities to gesture. Secondly, you'll be probably looking at it all the time, which will spoil the impression of your competence and thorough preparation for the presentation. Also avoid writing down the exact content of your presentation and learning it by heart, because when you forget a single word, the whole presentation will fall apart. In addition to this, everyone in the audience will hear that you learned it all by heart. Give yourself more flexibility and your presentation will be natural.

2. **Get rid of stage fright.** First of all, you need to know that you will make some errors during your presentation anyway. Maybe you will say something differently than you intended, or slightly change a fact that you used. This is perfectly normal and it happens to everyone. What is important, however, is that there is a 99% chance that NO ONE will even notice it. No matter what skills you have at the moment, you will probably sound a lot more informed than you think. Before your presentation, imagine that everything is going great, imagine how the audience is interested in what you say and how everyone applauds at the end. Before you start, do a few breathing exercises. The more you play, the better your presentation will be!

3. If possible, come **to the place of your presentation much earlier,** even before your listeners. Prepare the appropriate setting of chairs if you can, see how you feel while standing where you are going to speak. Then become a participant for a moment and sit in several places in the room—in the front, side and back of the room. See if everything will be visible from the perspective of a participant. On the basis of this knowledge, go back on stage and set everything so that the presentation goes smoothly and as you planned it.

4. **Clear your mind before getting on stage.** Stop thinking intensely about the material. When I started the adventure with public speaking, I would repeat the material I was going to present even one minute before starting the actual speech. I could not relax because of this and I still wasn't sure if I remembered everything. I quickly realized that everything goes much better when a few minutes before the start of my speech, I let it go completely and just trusted my subconscious. I also often

meditate to calm my mind and have a fully relaxed, chilled-out vibe. When the event starts, I present what comes to my mind, often according to the previously prepared plan, but sometimes I say completely unplanned things. So it is easier and better overall. Let it go right before the presentation, and put the plan and rehearsing aside.

5. **Take care of your posture.** Stand straight, putting the weight of the body on two slightly spaced legs. Keep your head high, so that your chin is pointing towards the horizon. This way you will give the impression of a confident person who is qualified in the subject. You should also work on your gestures. Use smooth gestures, which when used in an appropriate manner will picture what you are talking about. Gestures are the topic for a whole other book, but remember about the fact that the gestures should be peaceful, open and fluid. You shouldn't also gesture too high above your chest; it's best to keep your hands below the level of your chest, as some people see high gestures as overwhelming, annoying or explicit. Your body language should serve you as a powerful non-verbal message, which has great importance in the process of communication.

6. **Remember about facial expression.** Thanks to the appropriate use of this part of the body you can cause a lot of excitement in the audience, thanks to the so-called mirror neurons. That's why you should have a rich facial expression repertoire, smile often, raise your eyebrows and make expressions corresponding to what you are talking about. This will add depth and color to your presentation and make the audience understand what you have on your mind even better and faster.

7. **Modulate your voice.** Your vocal cords are a tool which can do absolute wonders when used properly. First of all, make sure that you speak clearly. Remember not to speak too fast, because people may not follow. The best idea is to record yourself on a voice recorder and then listen to yourself speak several times over. It will give you insight on what you can improve upon in your style of speaking. When performing in front of people, you need to change your voice frequently to evoke different emotional states in your listeners which will keep them from getting bored or distracted quickly. You can speak loudly at first only to start whispering a moment later to make them

curious. You can use different tones of your voice to accentuate different parts of the speech or to make people laugh. You can use pauses, so they start imagining what you wanted to tell them. The voice is one of the most crucial elements of public presentations, so put some time in practicing it and play with it all the time to achieve your goals.

8. **Look people in the eyes.** If it is a small group of people, you can look into the eyes of each person. If your group is larger, split it into some subgroups in your head and switch with your eyes between selected individuals in the group (then each member of the subgroup will have the impression that you're looking at them). Give your look and attention to all subgroups equally, jumping from one person to another. Don't do it too quickly—look in each person's eyes for about 3 seconds. At the beginning it might be quite a challenge for you, but you will get used to it with time. Thanks to this your listeners will feel like you are talking directly to them. It's very important if you want them to listen carefully.

The points below are the basics of a good performance. **Work on every one of these points, expanding your knowledge and skills.** At the earliest opportunity, apply them to your life, putting this advice into practice.

You might be still wondering about many things, such as how to build your authority as a speaker, how to put wise suggestions into your presentation or how to motivate listeners for active participation in your speech. You will find answers to all these questions below.

9. **Fit into the audience.** Before you start your presentation, consider who is going to be listening to you. What types of people are you are going to deal with? Will they be younger, older, students, sellers, buyers, CEO's or nuns? Think about the experiences, beliefs and values these people might have. Depending on who you will be talking to, you're going to use different examples, tell different stories and refer to different values. Also consider what kind of language they use in everyday life. You will be speaking completely differently to a group of friends than you would to a group of, for

example, vendors, bankers, rappers or teachers. Use their vocabulary and you will quickly establish a good rapport, thanks to which your listeners will quickly start feeling a stronger bond with you and will want to listen to you. The creation of such harmony gives amazing effects and creates amazing relationships between the professional speaker and the audience.

10. **Give motivation.** Without it, people won't need to listen to what you say. They need to know **why** this knowledge might be useful to them. The best situation occurs when there are two streams of motivation coming at them at once—both emotional and logical. At the beginning of your speech, you need to explain to them what the benefits will be (what can they learn, improve, etc.) if they listen to you carefully. Otherwise, they will feel no such need. If you build motivation skillfully, you will have their curiosity and attention provided for the rest of your presentation. Also, tell them **why** they need this knowledge. This element places your presentation's content in specific contexts of real life. Perhaps they will use it for building their career, relationships with people or even while shopping. Remember to always give them a good reason for listening to you. Do it at the beginning of your presentation, before you start to present the prepared material.

11. **Refer to your personal experiences.** Every one of us has thousands of diverse life experiences, which can be used as examples in the presentation. It could be even the most usual experiences—perhaps some time ago you were stuck in a traffic jam for a very long time, which helped you observe an interesting social phenomenon. Perhaps you were talking to a friend and saw a unique pattern in his behavior. It's all worth sharing. Why? Because when you refer to your experiences, two very important things happen. First of all, the audience knows that you know what you are talking about not only from books, but also from your own experience. Automatically you become an authority in the subject, so they want to listen to you more and believe in what you say. Secondly, they get tangible proof that what you're speaking about works and has its context in real life, as opposed to being just another abstract and boring theoretical concept. Therefore, you can write down all of your experiences which you want to share and use them during your performance.

12. **Tell stories.** Not only from your own life, but also these found or heard from someone else. Stories can be used to invoke various emotional states in your audience. One of the easiest emotional states to evoke is curiosity. It's also the state that you will need most during your presentation. If your audience is curious, they will listen carefully, craving more. It's good to include stories related to the topic that you are expanding on, but they don't have to be related directly. After you tell the story, you can explain what it has to do with your speech, even if the connection is slightly stretched. The story is not only supposed to illustrate your points, but also to evoke emotions. Learn the art of storytelling well, and play with your voice and body language. Sometimes you can pause just before the final moment of climax to make their curiosity grow even bigger. Then you can change topic and start telling about the main topic of your speech, leaving the ending of your story for later and keeping the audience interested and excited.

13. Whether or not the content of your presentation is a typical self-development topic, **install good stuff in your listeners' heads.** Believing in your authority, they will take most of the suggestions which you put in the presentation for granted. You might want to take advantage of this! You define your presentation with what you say. You don't want to say things like: "I know that you are already tired, but...," because then they will start to feel tired and this is not a good state for them to be in during your presentation. Instead, you can ask with a smile, "How are you?" This nonverbally assumes the fact that they are doing great. They will not probably start to jump with joy all of a sudden, but they will certainly start feeling better. You can also state that the topic of your presentation is very interesting. This works in your favor as opposed to a situation in which you would say, "I know that it's a bit boring, but...," which would lose the interest of each and every listener. Pick suggestions that you use carefully. We suggest something almost all the time, but usually we do it unconsciously.

14. **Never stop developing your public presentation skills.** The fastest way to improve leads, of course, is through frequent practice. However, if you do not have the possibility of making regular public speeches, you can always learn from other great speakers. You can model them (observe their verbal and non-verbal patterns and apply them to your own performances). You can use YouTube to look for world-class public

performers and watch their videos a few or a dozen or more times, carefully watching what they're doing. Then you need to see detailed elements of their style. Notice how they use their voice and how it affects listeners' emotions. What are they doing with their hands, what gestures do they normally use and in which context? Notice exactly what they are saying, what kind of language they are using, how are they introducing themselves and how they end their performances. By watching them so many times, you plant the seed of the new skills in your brain. To make it grow, step away from your computer and start to practice speaking in a similar manner to the person you have watched. Try to imitate their way of speaking. Do so with different speakers and gain new skills. Focus on only one speaker at a time and proceed to another one once you see all the patterns in their behaviors on stage. Don't worry, you won't be acting exactly like them and no one will call you a copycat; the new behaviors will blend with your own personality, giving you entirely unique vibe and style.

15. Ask for feedback. Ask your audience what you did well and what you could do better during your presentation. It is best to do it during an individual conversation with the participants; you can also ask them to send you an email with the feedback. This is the best way to learn, because you get the opportunity to look at yourself from a completely different perspective. The audience noticed the things that you did not notice and their opinion is the most valuable source of knowledge that will allow you to develop your skills. Ask them for honesty, because the less awkward they feel giving you feedback, the better it is for you. If you can, record your presentation with a video camera or even with a voice recorder. Such material is also a very valuable source of learning.

16. Have fun! Because if you have fun, your audience will have a good time too. It will make your presentation stay in their memory for a long time. Therefore, smile as often as you can, crack jokes, play with the entire process. Talk about the things that are most interesting for you. Even if the presentation is about an uninteresting topic, talk only about the most interesting things, and find some engaging examples. Be fascinated about what you say, and the audience will also be interested. Positive emotions during the presentation are crucial. Have fun with all what you are doing during a presentation!

Now it's time to practice. Write down each of these points on a sheet of paper, in the form of a single sentence so you can carry it with you. Thanks to this, you will always be aware of what you want to work with. Of course, do not use all of these 16 methods right at your next presentation. Choose 3 or 4 elements and practice them before the presentation so that you are able to successfully apply them into your life at the earliest opportunity. As soon as you are successful with those elements, select other ways and also start to practice them. Over time you will become a great public speaker, easily reaching the goals you seek for your presentations. People will listen to you with fascination and will remember your speeches for a long time.

Chapter 22: Create Unique Personality in Business

Who are you in your professional life? What label do you believe you have? Regardless of whether you present yourself as a salesperson, manager, accountant or small business owner, you need to know that there are specific cognitive schemes behind all these concepts or labels in the minds of other people.

If you want to build a strong personal brand based on your individual characteristics and unique skills, you may want to consider creating a new personality that will be defining you in the way that YOU choose.

Think of the name tags people use to describe themselves: manager, headhunter, trader, coach, freelancer, etc. Each of these concepts is linked with a particular type of social anchor. Not all associations are beneficial, so pinning such a pre-defined badge to your chest can sometimes be risky. Sometimes the associations following a particular title can be positive, and some other times it can be different. It all depends on your title, actual trends and who you are interacting with.

Is it enough to build a distinctive personal brand on the market? What about the fact that when you introduce yourself to someone you will still be a "business coach," "salesman" or "tax lawyer"? You will fall into one of the drawers in your interlocutor's head, where your title is already described in a more or less accurate way.

Even if a particular name on your badge sounds proud and you love wearing it, it will not allow you to create a strong brand based on your personal individuality.

There are a whole bunch of personal trainers, graphic designers, managers, physicians, IT engineers, sales people, lawyers, headhunters and so on—at some stage it can be really edifying to become one of them, but when you want to take a step further, you must go beyond the framework of your name tags. They are very limiting due to their predetermined place in the minds of people with whom you will communicate.

Imagine that someone introduces themselves to you. You ask, "What do you do?" and they reply: "I inspire people and show them how they can live better every day." The reaction for that response is likely to be quite different than if the answer was, "I'm a personal trainer." Thanks to this the person does not receive any predetermined label, but creates a new scheme in the interlocutor's mind, thereby **building their individual, personal brand.** Useful? You bet.

When I worked as an HR consultant, I conducted a training for one of the many European cosmetics companies. We came to the conclusion that the label of a "beautician" is a scheme that often makes it very hard to succeed in that industry. In that particular country, this identity was associated with rather average knowledge, little authority and low experience. It did not help in attracting new customers. We considered how we can create a new business personality while getting away from the "beautician" label at the same time.

The new cognitive scheme was supposed to present a thorough knowledge, substantial authority and high levels of experience. It was important to define ways in which employees of the company would build the new features of a freshly created identity. The first step was to get away from the "beautician" label—both in the minds of employees and when talking with clients. Then, a part of the training was about the technique of creating new features in the perception of the customer.

At the end, we called the new personality "*XYZ* Brand Specialist." Introducing themselves as beauticians, the employees would often lose the opportunity to establish a long-term cooperation right from the beginning.

Of course, creation of a new personality in business is always a little bit risky—if you do not do this consistently and actively, your new personality can be weaker than one of the already established job tags that you could also take. **It is therefore worth the time to remember that you should not take a name which you can't really "feel".**

Now, close your eyes and think about who you would be if there were no official jobs and labels by which you can specify the occupations of people in the world. How would you describe who you are in your professional life, maximally in two sentences?

If some kind of creative answer comes to your mind and you feel "That's it!"—perfect! **Start to use it and see what kind of reaction it evokes.**

Even if you have already assigned tag of, let's say, manager due to your professional position, it does not mean that you need to present yourself that way to other people.

If you do so all the time, your brand would be lost in the mass of other managers. You can be a manager in your professional hierarchy, but you can talk about yourself as of someone who **schedules the work of highly motivated people in order to make them act efficiently and effectively.** Sounds much better and more interesting.

Rethink the pride that comes from telling others about yourself as someone who is considered "important". Are you a director or president of a company? It's really cool, but does such a label tell people about who YOU really are? I don't think so.

Build your personal brand by showing your mission, your characteristics and your true personality. I like to think of myself as of a **guide** for people who are looking for their path. Some other times as a **person who inspires people** and shows them that it is possible to live a fulfilling and happy life. Recently, I've also been known as a **creator** who uses his creativity to enrich lives with new ideas. My personal brand varies depending on what I am focusing on at the moment.

Who do you think you are, considering what you do for a living? **What personal brand can you build?** Once you've established this, pay close attention to the reactions of people you introduce yourself to. Their different reactions will make you smile many times.

Bonus Chapter: Effective Networking

Think of your social network of professional relationships. Who accompanies you during your projects? Do you deal with everything on your own, or do you have people to whom, at any time, you can turn to for help and support?

This is important as every human you meet during conferences, seminars, various meetings or a tasty lunch break may be your next great business partner. How do we change a new relationship into a permanent and fruitful professional relationship?

The ability to create networks of contacts can turn out to be a big accelerator for realization of your goals. It is also a great opportunity to **expand your comfort zone**. Getting to know people from different industries will enrich your general knowledge and will be a great training of your interpersonal skills.

Networking is most useful in business when you are looking for business partners, employees or customers. It is also important for those working regular day jobs, when looking for new employers and job opportunities, to strengthen their position in the company or when establishing a new crucial professional relationship.

Here are my 11 tips that greatly help me in establishing new business relationships, often ending up with the effective joint implementation of a project.

1. Be where interesting people are. It's time to step out of your house! No excuses that you don't have time. Just go to a conference or live event. Look for a club bringing together the enthusiasts of particular business models, activities or professions. It is worth looking into LinkedIn's section of meetings. By selecting your city, you have the possibility to view the upcoming meetings, events, free lectures, conferences, etc. You can also try meetup.com.

2. Be aware of what kind of relationships you need. The biggest power in networking lies in the diverse network of contacts. Imagine that you are building a company, and your relationships support the process of establishing it step by step. When you need legal advice, you call your lawyer friend. If you have invoicing related questions, you write a short email to a colleague who is an accountant. Your friend who works in an interactive agency will design your company logo, because a few weeks ago you helped him with something else.

The more diverse your network of contacts gets, the easier it is to achieve your own goals.

3. Networking is not about handing out business cards all the time. This is the least important element. If someone wants to find you, in today's online world they will be able to do it even without this piece of paper. Despite the fact that most people's behavior suggests otherwise, the number of business cards handed out does not correlate with the number of established business contacts. Give people business cards only if it really creates a new opportunity. If there is no such need, just leave it in your pocket or pouch.

Although your business/contact cards are one of the least important elements of the jigsaw puzzle, if you choose to use them, of course they should be well prepared. Both the material on which they're printed as well as graphic design should show that you care about the details and the high quality of what you are doing. It would be best if you hired a professional graphic designer to come up with a simple and creative business card design for you. It is worth putting your photo on the card—this will reinforce the mnemonic trace of you. Always use the best quality paper for your contact cards. The devil's in the details.

4. Be the initiator. Don't let excuses stop you from acting! Most people are always open for exchanging a few sentences, and even for a longer chat. As the initiator of the conversations, you get the frame of a leader. Your conversation partner will have the impression that they're talking with a self-confident person for whom approaching people and building a network of contacts is a piece of cake. At conferences I often start conversations by asking a loose, non-binding question such as, "Which presentation have you enjoyed most so far?" Notice how that question directs an interlocutor to enter in a positive emotional state.

If you are at any conference and would like to speak to one of the speakers, simply go to them while they're on a break and ask them a few questions connected with their occupation.

Here's how you do it. You approach a person and say, "Hi, I'm (your name). What brought you here?" It's one of these universal questions that can always be asked. Then you wait for an answer, and reply, for instance: "How do you guys know each other?" (if there's more than one person, or you noticed that person talking to anyone else), or any other generic question. Then you follow up on what naturally comes in the conversation, for example, "That's cool, so what do you do?" A good idea might be to also make a statement on who that person is, if you have something positive to say. For example: "I get the impression that you are a very easy-going and relaxed, but yet a very professional person and you're really serious about what you do." Of course, you shouldn't use that if you just started talking to someone and don't know anything at all about them, but if you've heard something about that person before, been talking for a few minutes, or that person was giving a lecture, speech or presentation, that's a great way to lead the conversation. Always remember to ask just a couple of questions and then make a statement with what they said, as no one likes to be interrogated.

If you want or have to exit conversation, just say, "It was a pleasure to meet you, thanks for chatting and see you around!"

Don't hold yourself back! People will be really happy to talk to you (even famous people and main event guests, if they have enough time) and it may emerge into something really precious and important. Easy-peasy.

5. Put relationship before profits. It is surprising how often people focus solely on the possibility of achieving benefits from relationships, both in casual relationships and professional networking. When building a network of contacts, the most important thing is the relationship with another human being. **People like doing business with people they know and like.** Therefore, the option of cooperating or exchanging favors in one way or another should be put on the back burner.

If you have the opportunity to speak with a newly met person only for a few minutes, focus on getting to know each other. If you want, try to arrange a next meeting at the end of the conversation, but wait a little bit until you roll the heavy cannons out. When

I meet energetic people full of ideas, I want first to get to know them better. I won't decide on working with someone I do not really know.

When you have some very important business on your mind and you really can't wait to share it, do not beat around the bush—be straightforward and do not try to come by using "magic bullets," "smoothly" and "accidentally" bumping into the topic that interest you the most. Networking often takes the form of a purely business conversation, without a real foundation of personal relationship. Sometimes it can be okay, but it will be much harder to build a long-term cooperation on that foundation.

6. Focus on the human element. Open up to people. Listen to them carefully and take notes in your mind to remember what is important for them in their life. Ask them interesting questions. Let them tell you about their projects, passions or dreams.

Don't think you have to talk much to make people like you. This is an incorrect assumption. The ability to listen is MUCH more important here. Be sincerely interested, and you'll make the impression of a trustworthy interlocutor.

Tell them about your passions and projects when you are asked about them, if there is a perfect moment to do it, but if you wait for a moment when you can finally put in the story about yourself, you become distracted and lose the ability to truly concentrate on what your interlocutor says.

After all, the contents of your conversation is not what really matters, it's about the quality of your contact. If something sparks, you will surely feel it.

7. Always aim at win-win. This means intentionally leading to situations where both sides benefit, not only you. In addition, be the first who **adds value**. Before the actual opportunity to establish new business relationship, you should have a list of things that you can offer these people to improve their situation. It can be knowledge, contacts, skills, time, advice and even a product or service. It is possible that during the conversation it turns out that your interlocutors have a problem or challenge ahead of them. If possible, try to help them, sharing with them your perspective, ideas or resources. This is how Caldini's norm of reciprocity works. People whom you helped will feel the strong urge to help you.

8. Be honest. Authenticity is a rare feature which can help you to establish really fruitful professional relationships. Do not try to build a network of contacts based on a personality that is not really yours or one that is pretending to be someone else. Going into cooperation with someone who thinks that you are someone else than you really are is not the best idea. I'm not necessarily talking about just saying that you're a rocket scientist when you're really a clerk, but rather telling someone things just to show yourself from a good angle, but far from the actual truth.

Even if you think that lying or saying half-truths in a given situation will be good for you because, for instance, you will sell more products, or you'll get a faster promotion, do not entertain this illusion—in many cases it will ultimately turn against you. Solid businesses are always created on the foundation of true and honest relationships.

9. Take care of the already established contacts. This does not mean that you have to meet with each person once a week. It is important, however, that once a relationship has been established, it shouldn't not be completely neglected, because it will eventually shrink and vanish. It's always been a big challenge for me because of the number of projects I usually deal with, but I found that it does not necessarily require large amounts of time.

You can go with little follow-ups or "reminder" e-mails. Write a short message and ask what's going on. Minimalist version: "Hey, we met two days ago at the *XYZ* in *ABC*. How is your first day of a new work week? You are probably hustling to launch your new project soon. Thanks a lot for the great tips on *QQQ*. It was nice to meet you and I hope to talk to you face to face in the near future. In case I could somehow lend you a helpful hand, let me know." You can also propose a concrete date of appointment or a brief conversation on Skype.

10. Have a neat record of your contacts. Just a simple spreadsheet in Excel is enough. Divide it into categories so you can quickly find the person you are looking for. Save all the relevant information: name and surname, phone number, e-mail address, web sites, and if necessary, any additional comments. Add a small photo of that person if you can.

From time to time, browse your registry to keep up to date—it will be much easier for you to decide whether it would be worth contacting someone, if you did not do so for a long period of time.

11. Find people close to you with a large number of contacts. They can be a sort of "door" to new relationships. Take a look, and maybe you already have someone like this in your surroundings. In a situation where you need a person working in a specific occupation, simply ask about it. Remember about the classic principle of reciprocity and also share your contacts.

Remember—**always put people and real, sincere relationships with them in first place.** Let the potential profits and benefits remain on the second plan, and they will come with time.

Conclusion

It doesn't take rocket science to figure out that effective communication is the most important skill to learn and master as a human being. I truly hope this book was able to bring you closer to this goal and to inspire you. Remember, the most effective communicators on this planet (historical spiritual and new movement leaders, politicians and dictators with big impacts, hero spies, the best teachers, legendary seducers, celebrities loved by masses, big company owners, good parents, popular YouTubers, writers, journalists, psychotherapists, stand-up comedians, actors...) were not usually just born like that! Communication is a skill like any other and it can be trained. If others can do it, so can you!

I wish you all the best on your journey and hope you will get there soon! Remember: you are who you stick with, so the sooner you start hanging out with people who also want to be effective communicators, the better. Look for your local Toastmasters or rhetoric group, practice with a mirror and camera, read more books about social psychology and body language and never stop growing! The main prize is totally worth it! I believe in you!

One last thing before you go—can I ask you a favor? I need your help! If you like this book, could you please share your experience on Amazon and write an honest review? It will take just a minute of your time (I will be happy even with one sentence!), but would be a GREAT help for me.

Here's link: https://tinyurl.com/reviewmycommbook

Since I'm not a well-established author and I don't have powerful people and big publishing companies supporting me, I read every single review and jump with joy like a little kid every time my readers comment on my books and give me their honest feedback! If I was able to inspire you in any way, please let me know! It will also help me get my books in front of more people looking for new ideas and useful knowledge.

If you did not enjoy the book or had a problem with it, please don't hesitate to contact me at contact@mindfulnessforsuccess.com and tell me how I can improve it to provide more value and more knowledge to my readers. I'm constantly working on my books to make them better and more helpful.

Thank you and good luck! I believe in you and I wish you all the best on your new journey!

Your friend,

Ian

My Free Gift to You

Discover How to Get Rid of Stress & Anxiety and Reach Inner Peace in 20 Days or Less!

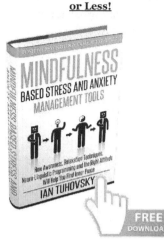

To help speed up your personal transformation, I have prepared a special gift for you!

Download my full, 120-page e-book "Mindfulness Based Stress and Anxiety Management Tools" (Value: $9.99) for free by clicking here.

Moreover, by becoming my subscriber, you will be the first one to **get my new books for only $0.99,** during their short two-day promotional launch. **I passionately write about**: social dynamics, career, Neuro-Linguistic Programming, goal achieving, positive psychology and philosophy, life hacking, meditation and becoming the most awesome version of yourself. Additionally, once a week I will send you insightful tips and **free e-book offers** to keep you on track on your journey to becoming the best you!

That's my way of saying **"thank you"** to my new and established readers and helping you grow. I hate spam and e-mails that come too frequently—**you will never receive more than one email a week! Guaranteed.**

Just follow this link:

https://tinyurl.com/mindfulnessgift

Hey there like-minded friends, let's get connected!

Don't hesitate to visit:

-My Blog: www.mindfulnessforsuccess.com

-My Facebook fanpage: https://www.facebook.com/mindfulnessforsuccess

-My Twitter: https://twitter.com/mindfulness78

Twitter handle: @Mindfulness4Success
-My Instagram profile: https://instagram.com/mindfulnessforsuccess

I hope to see you there!

Recommended Reading for You:

If you are interested in Self-Development, NLP, Psychology, Social Dynamics, PR, Soft Skills and related topics, you might be interested in previewing or downloading my other books:

Natural Confidence Training: How to Develop Healthy Self-Esteem and Deep Self-Confidence to Be Successful and Become True Friends with Yourself

Lack of self-confidence and problems with unhealthy self-esteem are usually the reason why smart, competent and talented people never achieve a satisfying life, a life that should easily be possible for them.

Think about your childhood.
At the age of four or five, there weren't too many things that you considered impossible, right?
You weren't bothered or held back by any kind of criticism; you stayed indifferent to what other people thought of you. An ugly stain on your sweater, or even worse, on your leggings, was not considered a problem or an obstacle.

You could run on a crowded beach absolutely nude, laughing, go swimming in a city fountain and then play in the sandbox with strawberry ice cream smeared in your hair. Nothing and no one could stop you from saying what you wanted to say, even the silliest things. **There was no shame in your early childhood;** you loved yourself and everyone else.

Can you remember it?
What happened to us?

Parents, teachers, preachers and media **stuffed certain beliefs into your head**, day after day for many years. These beliefs and attitudes **robbed you of your natural, inborn confidence.**
Maybe it was one traumatic experience of some kind that changed you, or maybe it was a slow process that lasted for years. One thing is certain—lacking confidence is not your natural, default state. **It brings you down and now you have to unlearn it.**

Can you name even a single situation in life where high confidence isn't useful?

... Right?

Confidence is not useful only in everyday life and casual situations. Do you really want to fulfill your dreams, or do you just want to keep chatting about them with your friends, until one day you wake up as a grumpy, old, frustrated person?

Big achievements require brave and fearless actions. If you want to act bravely, you need to be confident.
Along with lots of useful, practical exercises, this book will provide you with plenty of new information that will help you understand what confidence problems really come down to. And this is the most important and the saddest part, because most people do not truly recognize the root problem, and that's why they get poor results.

In this book you will read about:
-How, when and why society robs us all of natural confidence and healthy self-esteem.
-What kind of social and psychological traps you need to avoid to feel much calmer, happier and more confident.
-What "natural confidence" means and how it becomes natural.
-What "self-confidence" really is and what it definitely isn't (as opposed to what most people think!).
-How your mind hurts you when it really just wants to help you, and how to stop the process.
-What different kinds of fear we feel, where they come from and how to defeat them.
-How to have a great relationship with yourself.
-What beliefs and habits you should have and cultivate to succeed.
-How to use stress to boost your inner strength.
-Effective and ineffective ways of building healthy self-esteem.
-How mindfulness and meditation help boost, cultivate and maintain your natural confidence.
-Why the relation between self-acceptance and stress is so crucial.
-How to stay confident in professional situations.
-How to protect your self-esteem when life brings you down and how to deal with criticism and jealousy.
-How to use neuro-linguistic programming, imagination, visualizations, diary entries and your five senses to re-program your subconscious and get rid of "mental viruses" and detrimental beliefs that actively destroy your natural confidence and healthy self-esteem.

In the last part of the book you will find 15 of the most effective, proven and field-tested strategies and exercises that help people transform their lives.

Take the right action and start changing your life for the better today!

Direct Buy Link to Amazon Kindle Store:
https://tinyurl.com/IanConfidenceTraining

https://tinyurl.com/IanConfidencePaperback

Emotional Intelligence Training: A Practical Guide to Making Friends with Your Emotions and Raising Your EQ

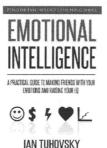

Do you believe your life would be healthier, happier and even better, if you had more practical strategies to regulate your own emotions?

Most people agree with that.

Or, more importantly:

Do you believe you'd be healthier and happier if everyone who you live with had the strategies to regulate their emotions?

...Right?

The truth is not too many people actually realize what EQ is really all about and what causes its popularity to grow constantly.

Scientific research conducted by many American and European universities prove that the **"common" intelligence responses account for less than 20% of our life achievements and successes, while the other over 80% depends on emotional intelligence.** To put it roughly: **either you are emotionally intelligent, or you're doomed to mediocrity, at best.**

As opposed to the popular image, emotionally intelligent people are not the ones who react impulsively and spontaneously, or who act lively and fiery in all types of social environments.

Emotionally intelligent people are open to new experiences, can show feelings adequate to the situation, either good or bad, and find it easy to socialize with other people and establish new contacts. They handle stress well, say "no" easily, realistically assess the achievements of themselves or others and are not afraid of constructive criticism and taking calculated risks. **They are the people of success.** Unfortunately, this perfect model of an emotionally intelligent person is extremely rare in our modern times.

Sadly, nowadays, **the amount of emotional problems in the world is increasing at an alarming rate.** We are getting richer, but less and less happy. Depression, suicide, relationship breakdowns, loneliness of choice, fear of closeness, addictions—this is clear evidence that we are getting increasingly worse when it comes to dealing with our emotions.

Emotional intelligence is a SKILL, and can be learned through constant practice and training, just like riding a bike or swimming!

This book is stuffed with lots of effective exercises, helpful info and practical ideas.

Every chapter covers different areas of emotional intelligence and shows you, **step by step**, what exactly you can do to **develop your EQ** and become the **better version of yourself**.

I will show you how freeing yourself from the domination of left-sided brain thinking can contribute to your inner transformation—**the emotional revolution that will help you redefine who you are and what you really want from life!**

<u>**In This Book I'll Show You:**</u>

- What Is Emotional Intelligence and What Does EQ Consist of?
- How to **Observe and Express** Your Emotions
- How to **Release Negative Emotions** and **Empower the Positive Ones**
- How to Deal with Your **Internal Dialogues**
- How to **Deal with the Past**
- **How to Forgive** Yourself and How to Forgive Others
- How to Free Yourself from **Other People's Opinions and Judgments**
- What Are "Submodalities" and How Exactly You Can Use Them to **Empower Yourself** and **Get Rid of Stress**
- The Nine Things You Need to **Stop Doing to Yourself**
- How to Examine Your Thoughts
- **Internal Conflicts** Troubleshooting Technique
- The Lost Art of Asking Yourself the Right Questions and **Discovering Your True Self!**
- How to Create Rich Visualizations
- LOTS of practical exercises from the mighty arsenal of psychology, family therapy, NLP etc.
- **And many, many more!**

Direct Buy Link to Amazon Kindle Store:
https://tinyurl.com/IanEQTrainingKindle

Paperback version on Createspace: https://tinyurl.com/ianEQpaperback

Meditation for Beginners: How to Meditate (as an Ordinary Person!) to Relieve Stress and Be Successful

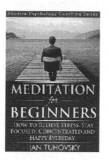

Meditation doesn't have to be about crystals, hypnotic folk music and incense sticks! **Forget about sitting in unnatural and uncomfortable positions while going, "Ommmmm...."** It is not necessarily a club full of yoga masters, Shaolin monks, hippies and new-agers.

It is a super useful and universal practice which can improve your overall brain performance and happiness. When meditating, you take a step back from actively thinking your thoughts, and instead see them for what they are. The reason why meditation is helpful in reducing stress and attaining peace is that it gives your over-active consciousness a break.

Just like your body needs it, your mind does too!

I give you the gift of peace that I was able to attain through present moment awareness.

Direct Buy Link to Amazon Kindle Store:
https://tinyurl.com/IanMeditationGuide

Paperback version on Createspace: http://tinyurl.com/ianmeditationpaperback

Zen: Beginner's Guide: Happy, Peaceful and Focused Lifestyle for Everyone

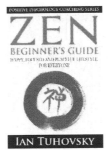

Contrary to popular belief, Zen is not a discipline reserved for monks practicing Kung Fu. Although there is some truth to this idea, Zen is a practice that is applicable, useful and pragmatic for anyone to study regardless of what religion you follow (or don't follow).

Zen is the practice of studying your subconscious and **seeing your true nature.** The purpose of this work is to show you how to apply and utilize the teachings and essence of Zen in everyday life in the Western society. I'm not really an "absolute truth seeker" unworldly type of person—I just believe in practical plans and blueprints that actually help in living a better life. Of course I will tell you about the origin of Zen and the traditional ways of practicing it, but I will also show you my side of things, my personal point of view and translation of many Zen truths into a more "contemporary" and practical language.

It is a "modern Zen lifestyle" type of book.

What You Will Read About:

• Where Did Zen Come from? - A short history and explanation of Zen
• What Does Zen Teach? - The major teachings and precepts of Zen
• Various Zen meditation techniques that are applicable and practical for everyone!
• The Benefits of a Zen Lifestyle
• What Zen Buddhism is NOT?
• How to Slow Down and Start Enjoying Your Life
• How to Accept Everything and Lose Nothing
• Why Being Alone Can Be Beneficial
• Why Pleasure Is NOT Happiness
• Six Ways to Practically Let Go
• How to De-clutter Your Life and Live Simply
• "Mindfulness on Steroids"
• How to Take Care of Your Awareness and Focus
• Where to Start and How to Practice Zen as a Regular Person
• And many other interesting concepts...
I invite you to take this journey into the peaceful world of Zen Buddhism with me today!

Direct Buy Link to Amazon Kindle Store: https://tinyurl.com/IanZenGuide

Paperback version on Createspace: http://tinyurl.com/ianzenpaperback

Buddhism: Beginner's Guide: Bring Peace and Happiness to Your Everyday Life

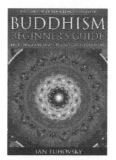

Buddhism is one of the most practical and simple belief systems on this planet, and it has greatly helped me on my way to become a better person in every aspect possible. In this book I will show you what happened and how it was.

No matter if you are totally green when it comes to Buddha's teachings or maybe you have already heard something about them—this book will help you systematize your knowledge and will inspire you to learn more and to take steps to make your life positively better!

I invite you to take this beautiful journey into the graceful and meaningful world of Buddhism with me today!

Direct link to Amazon Kindle Store: https://tinyurl.com/IanBuddhismGuide

Paperback version on Createspace: http://tinyurl.com/ianbuddhismpaperback

Speed Reading: How to Read 3-5 Times Faster and Become an Effective Learner

No matter if your objective is to **do great during your university exams,** become a **bestselling writer** or start **your own business,** you will have to read A LOT, and I mean it. Reading takes time. **Time is our most valuable asset**—nothing new here. You can always make money or meet new friends, but **you will never be able to "make time."** The only way to succeed and have a happy life without regrets is to use it wisely and **learn how to manage and save it.**

In this book, I will take you through the dynamics of speed reading in a way you may have never imagined before. I'm here to preach the need for speed reading and make use of some of the principles that can steer your knowledge and productivity in the right direction.

Learn How to Read 5 Times Faster, Remember Much More and Save Massive Time!

In This Book You Will Read About:
- The History of Speed Reading
- Popular Speed Reading Myths
- **Environment and Preparation**
- How to Measure Your Reading Speed
- **Key Speed Reading Techniques**
- Reading Tips for Computer and Tablet
- Common Reading Mistakes to Avoid
- Easy and Effective Memory/Learning Techniques
- **Dealing with Tests and Diagrams**
- **Practical Exercises and Eye Adjustments**
- Useful Links and Ideas
- Diet

- How to Track Your Progress
- Proper Motivation and Mindset

Direct link to Amazon Kindle Store: https://tinyurl.com/IanSpeedReading

Paperback version on Createspace: http://tinyurl.com/ianreadingpaperback

About The Author

Author's blog: www.mindfulnessforsuccess.com

Amazon Author Page: http://www.amazon.com/author/iantuhovsky/

Hi! I'm Ian...

. . . and I am interested in life. I am in the study of having an awesome and passionate life, which I believe is within the reach of practically everyone. I'm not a mentor or a guru. I'm just a guy who always knew there was more than we are told. I managed to turn my life around from way below my expectations to a really satisfying one, and now I want to share this fascinating journey with you so that you can do it, too.

I was born and raised somewhere in Eastern Europe, where Polar Bears eat people on the streets, we munch on snow instead of ice cream and there's only vodka instead of tap water, but since I make a living out of several different businesses, I move to a new country every couple of months. I also work as an HR consultant for various European companies.

I love self-development, traveling, recording music and providing value by helping others. I passionately read and write about social psychology, sociology, NLP, meditation, mindfulness, eastern philosophy, emotional intelligence, time management, communication skills and all of the topics related to conscious self-development and being the most awesome version of yourself.

Breathe. Relax. Feel that you're alive and smile. And never hesitate to contact me!

Made in the USA
Charleston, SC
26 February 2017